CRY OUT!

CRY OUT!

P. E. Quinn

ABINGDON PRESS
NASHVILLE

CRY OUT!

Copyright © 1984 Abingdon Press

Library of Congress Cataloging in Publication Data
QUINN, P. E. (PHIL E.), 1950-
  Cry out!
  Bibliography: p.
  1. Quinn, P. E. (Phil E.), 1950-   . 2. Abused children—United
States) Biography. 3. Children, Adopted— United States—Biogra-
phy. 4. Broken homes—United States—Case studies. 5. Foster
parents—United States—Case studies. 6. Child abuse—United
States. 7. Child abuse—Services—United States. I. Title.
HV741.Q56   1984   362.7'044   83-27536

ISBN 0-687-10015-1

MANUFACTURED BY THE PARTHENON PRESS AT
NASHVILLE, TENNESSEE, UNITED STATES OF AMERICA

This book is dedicated to my children
Deanna and Jonathan
and yours—
may they each be blessed with
joyful memories of
childhood

[Contents]

[Acknowledgments]

the Courage to face alone at last
the Risk of reliving a tormented past;
the Yielding to a role long cast—
    I owe to many along the way.

the Opportunity at last to share;
the Understanding, its strength to dare;
the Truth I know as loving care—
    I owe to few, only yesterday.

My sincere thanks to Sabrina Ellis, Elaine Pike, and Cathy Stuard for their long, tedious labor typing and retyping the manuscript. Their gifts of time and talent made my task much easier.

To all the employees of the Jesse Holman Jones Hospital, especially my friends in the business office, I owe a special word of thanks. Their unfailing support and enthusiasm fueled my own at times of greatest need. Their gift cannot be measured; it can only be witnessed in this completed manuscript.

No greater debt do I owe than to those dear friends who in their caring accompanied my pilgrimage through every word, every page of the writing of this book, every day, from beginning to end: Wanda Peterson, Mary Ann Harned, Linda Allen, and especially Marilyn Worsham and Senthia Grant. They gave me inspiration in times of despair, strength in moments of weakness, courage to continue when fear threatened to overpower me. They listened to me, encouraged me, uplifted me. They even cried with me. There is not a word to describe their gift to me nor my gratefulness to them.

Lastly, to Dr. Joe Bragg, Jr., Mary Ruth Howes, and especially LaVerna Smith, without each of whom this book would never have been written or published, I pay my greatest tribute. For they are my mentors.

P.E. Quinn
Nashville, Tennessee
March 21, 1983

[Preface]

In this book, I shall call myself Peter. I was a victim of severe abuse and neglect as a child. Like many others raised in an environment of danger, violence, and degradation, I developed and survived as a social mutant. Childhood for most people is remembered as a time in which the only limit of possibility was the limit of imagination; a time of carefree irresponsibility, of unending hours at play in an ever-expanding playground, of warmth, love, and security in a home with parents who were always there, of hopes, dreams, and fantasies as real as life itself; a time in which the most important thing in life was the freedom to be a child.

Most of my childhood memories are of a different sort. Since I was six survival has been my primary life goal—physical and emotional survival. As a child I existed as a human chameleon, constantly changing to protect myself from the ever-changing face of danger that always seemed a part of my life. Most people who knew me as a child and adolescent thought my behavior deviant, maladaptive, or pathological. By their standards they were right. By most standards they were right. But by the only standard that mattered to me then—the standard of survival—they were wrong. Given the circumstances in which I lived, most of my thinking and behavior was not only appropriate, but a necessary adaptation for self-preservation. If I had to lie to avoid a beating, I lied. If I had to steal to eat, I stole. If I had to destroy to avoid destruction, I wreaked havoc. If I had to inflict pain to avoid pain, then I made people suffer. I only wanted to survive, in the only way I knew how, the danger that threatened daily to destroy me—my parents.

The pain and suffering caused by child abuse do not end with the final blow. Although the body may heal and show only scars, the emotional wounds often fester over long years of psychological denial and repression, providing a constant source of resurging pain in an already troubled and desperate life. Failure, frustration, fear, anger, and despair commonly characterize the adult life of a child abuse survivor.

Although the names, dates, and locations in the story you are about to read have been changed so as not to perpetuate the grief and horror of memories that rightfully belong in the past, the story in its entirety is true—painfully true. Every incident did, in fact, occur. My only reason for recounting these experiences is an attempt to cry out for mercy and compassion on behalf of the thousands of children in our country who even today experience the misery of abuse in their childhood years—years in which children, muted and helpless, suffer within the prison of their endless, living nightmares.

Although the details of the story are my life experience, the story is similar to thousands of others. It might just as well be your story, or that of someone you know. I have no special place among those who have suffered and survived. I am but a statistic. Just another victim. One of thousands. But more fortunate than most, I suppose, because I have been set free of my past; free to turn my eyes to the future, to my children, to the living of each day freed from the grip of human madness. Many survivors are not so fortunate. Mental hospitals, prisons, and graveyards claim many at an early age. Those who escape this doom can never escape entirely their memories.

The purpose of this book is not to inflict pain, but to

relieve it; not to condemn, but to exhort; not to frighten, but to inspire. I do not want to suggest that all foster and adoptive families are potentially or actually abusive. Onthe contrary, most provide an excellent home environment for some very fortunate children. However, there are those families which do become abusive. My sincere hope is that this book will make a difference in one such family and at least in one child's life—if not in the life of your own child, then perhaps in the life of the child next door.

It is only appropriate, then, as I represent the nameless, that I too remain nameless. I shall call myself Peter, not because I want to hide my history, but rather to draw your attention away from me, an adult survivor, toward the children who so desperately need our help. Only by writing in the third person could I cope with these horrible memories to make possible your experience of them through the eyes of a child.

CRY OUT!

[PART I]
The Family

* * * *

Peter was the third of five children born in as many years. His parents, Mike and Carol, had been married less than a year when the first child was born.

Mike was of American Indian descent, and he spent most of his youth on a reservation. His parents pushed him into making education an important priority in his life. Successfully completing high school, he entered college on an ROTC scholarship. In September 1943, his ROTC unit was placed on active duty. He was assigned to the Ninty-ninth Army Infantry Division as a combat engineer. Shortly after the Malmédy Massacre on December 17, 1944, he was wounded and sent first to Paris, then to London, for convalescence.

There, in a small hospital on the outskirts of the bombed-out city, he met his future wife. As a young woman, Carol had joined the British Army nursing corps early in the war. She was bred of sturdy English stock, aristocratic and sophisticated, her centuries-old family commanding a respectful place in the flow of British history.

Despite their divergent backgrounds, Mike and Carol were drawn together out of the frightening uncertainties of a world at war as she tended his wounds and he tended her lonely fears. They were married in 1946 and came to America to settle in a small community near his home reservation. On the promise of love and happiness, Carol left her home, family, and roots in England.

She became totally involved with the raising of her children while he worked to support the family and reentered college. The simultaneous pressures of work and school, coupled with his long hours away from home, placed extraordinary strain on the marriage. Soon they were in open rebellion against each other, and the fighting began.

[Chapter One]

The darkness of another lonely night smothered the small bedroom like a cold, moist blanket. Occasionally light from a passing car would penetrate the gloom and for a moment the bare walls would come alive with grotesque and ghostly shadows, only to be plunged into a deeper darkness a moment later. The room was heavy with silence. Nothing moved.

On any other night the small boy sitting like a statue beside the window would have been hiding from his imagination under a pile of blankets on the bed. But not tonight. There was something more important taking place that held his full attention; something even more frightening than the ghoulish fantasies of a child afraid of the dark. Staring blindly into the raindrops forming on the window glass, he sat absorbed in the nightmare taking place in another part of the house.

All evening long his mother and father had been fighting. It began at the dinner table when the family sat down to eat. Slowly at first, accusing questions and caustic replies. The kids knew it was coming. They could feel the tension mounting between their parents. Then, in a sudden burst of anger, they were sent to their rooms. The skirmish exploded into full-fledged battle; like warring ships the parents pummeled each other with barrage after barrage of angry words. Though painfully silent now, the air still rang with the bitterness of their voices.

Six-year-old Peter heard every word and understood none of them. It was the uncontrolled rage behind the words that frightened him so much. He had no idea what might have happened to cause his parents to be so angry. But with a child's instinct for such things, he knew they were trying to hurt each other. He was torn between the desire to defend his parents from each other and the urge to run and hide from them for fear they might turn their anger upon him. He both loved them and feared them. Even more, he needed them to stop fighting.

As he strained to hear what might happen next, Peter knew there was nothing he could do to stop what was happening in the other room. With a deep sigh the troubled boy sat frightened and alone in the cold prison of his empty bedroom hoping that the fight would soon be over.

Always before, his mother would slip away long enough to tuck him and his brothers into bed and assure them that everything was going to be all right. How he yearned now to hear her light steps coming down the hallway to bring him that message of comfort!

It had not always been this way. There had been a time when his parents did not fight. Peter could remember happy days at home, times of loving one another warmly and openly, laughing and playing together like a real family. There were family gatherings at Thanksgiving and Christmas, birthday parties, Sunday school, and good-night hugs. His father would sometimes tuck him snugly into bed. And if he was really good, his father might even read him a bedtime story about Br'er Rabbit and Br'er Fox. How he loved those special times! Long walks in the park, the cherished penny and peppermint stick given out on Saturday mornings, the long Sunday drives in the country. His father would often stop the car at a roadside hamburger stand on their way to grandpa's farm and buy milkshakes for the family. Everyone else liked strawberry and vanilla, but Peter liked chocolate. He felt different and kind of special every time his father brought the milkshakes to the car and only one was chocolate—his!

After handing out the other six so that only the chocolate milkshake remained unclaimed, his father would turn to his mother with a puzzled look on his face and exclaim, "They must have given us one too many milkshakes, momma! Looky here, everyone has one and there is still one left over. Besides, who in this family likes chocolate? Yuk!"

Peter, sitting snugly between his older brother and sister in the backseat, would be nearly bursting with anticipation by this time. Winking at his wife with a feigned confusion clouding his face, the children's father would finally shrug carelessly and make a move to get out of the car and return the unclaimed milkshake. That was Peter's cue.

"It's mine, daddy, it's mine!" he would shout excitedly, bouncing up and down on the seat. "I like chocolate! Please, daddy, I like chocolate!"

The banter would continue for a moment between Peter and his father until at last the coveted milkshake would be surrendered to the eager and happy boy.

Peter loved this game with his father. It was something special just between the two of them. It made him feel special.

But that was a long time ago, before the fighting started. Now his father was home infrequently and only for brief visits. He would pay little attention to Peter and his younger brothers, but the two older children, David and Sharon, would dash headlong into his arms at the first sign of his entering the room. Chattering excitedly they would command his attention throughout the visit. Trailing after his older brother and sister, Peter would try desperately to get his father's attention. But try as he might, he could not compete with his older siblings. He would give up and climb quietly into the chair near the door and watch them playing together on the living room floor. Obviously the older two were the father's favorites. With eyes bright and eager, Peter would wait patiently for his turn that never came.

After awhile his father would tire of the play, give them each one last hug, talk to his mother for a moment, and then leave. Occasionally he would ruffle Peter's hair as he moved quickly past the anxious boy and out the door.

Going to the front window Peter would watch his father's car leave the driveway and disappear down the street. After a moment he would turn from the window, move slowly to his mother and climb into her lap. Turning his troubled, searching eyes to hers, the child would ask in his small voice once more, "Momma, don't I have a daddy, too?"

The times when his father was able to stay at home for longer periods were filled usually with quarreling, drinking, and angry shouting until again he would leave. No more walks in the park or drives in the country, no more hugs or bedtime stories, and no more chocolate milkshakes.

Nothing was the same. Even his mother had changed. She would often sleep most of the day or watch television for long hours at a time. Sometimes Peter would find her crying into the pillow on the bed. He worried that she did not laugh and play with them much any more. She always seemed so tired. Sitting close beside her on the couch he could feel the sadness and quiet desperation out of which she now lived.

Now, after several weeks' absence, his father had returned home again. Peter had been jubilant with the hope that maybe he would stay this time. But then the fighting started again.

A small voice from inside the room began reaching slowly into Peter's thoughts, the voice of his younger brother, Jimmy.

"Peter?"

Peter moved across the room and stood beside the bed. Even in the darkness he could see the vague forms of his two younger brothers huddled close together on the bed.

"You guys are supposed to be asleep," he answered. "Momma's gonna be mad."

"I can't go to sleep," whispered Jimmy. "I ain't sleepy no more, Peter."

"Me neither," cried Bobby, beginning to whimper.

Peter was two years older than Bobby and less than a year older than Jimmy. With his older brother and sister locked in their bedroom across the hall, Peter somehow felt responsible for his younger brothers. It hurt him to see them so scared and upset. After a moment he moved closer to his crying brother, placed his arm about his shoulders as he had seen his mother do, and tried to comfort him. For a long time the three boys sat on the bed helplessly drawn closer together by the horrible uncertainties of that eternal night.

"Is momma and daddy fighting again, Peter?" Jimmy asked.

"Yeah, I guess so."

"Peter?"

"What?"

"It's bad this time, ain't it, Peter?" Peter was surprised by his brother's question and could not answer him.

"Peter?" the concerned voice of Jimmy called out once more.

"What?"

"What's going to happen this time, Peter?" Again receiving no answer from his older brother, Jimmy began to cry. "Peter, I want momma! I'm scared."

Peter tried to comfort them. "It's OK, you guys. Everything will be all right in the morning. You'll see." With these familiar words the whimpering stopped. That was what momma always told them. "Now you guys lie back down and go to sleep."

The two boys obeyed, sliding under the covers until only their eyes and the tops of the heads were visible. Within moments the restless tossing and turning stopped. The deep, rhythmic breathing of the two shadows told Peter his brothers had finally fallen asleep.

Returning to the chair beside the window, Peter sat down. Leaning forward, he watched as the window began to fog up from the warmth of his breath on the cold glass. For a moment it held his attention. Then he heard the footsteps. They were coming down the hallway toward his bedroom! Maybe the fighting was over and they were coming to tuck him into bed! Suddenly excited, he raced to the door to meet his mother. Then he heard his father's muffled voice, deep and low. He had been drinking. Peter could tell by the way the words slurred together and how he followed his hand down the wall to steady himself. Peter froze in his tracks, suddenly frightened again. He listened intently as the bedroom door across the hall burst open, banging hard against the wall. He could hear the whispers of his brother and sister as they were ushered out of the room and down the hall.

"Where are we going, daddy?" his sister was asking, her voice trembling.

"Daddy, why is momma crying? Is something wrong?" asked David when there was no answer to his sister's question. "Is momma coming with us, daddy?"

"You kids hush!" commanded their father with a heavy voice. "Now run and jump in the car. I'll be there in a minute."

Peter moved quickly back to the window and watched his brother and sister leave the front porch and climb together into the backseat of the car parked in the driveway.

The silence in the living room was shattered by his mother screaming. A lamp crashed to the floor amidst the sound of scuffling and hysterical screams. The front door opened and slammed shut.

Biting hard on his quivering lip, Peter could not stop the flow of silent tears streaming down his face. He sat with his arms wrapped tightly about his shaking body, his every sense flooded with painful tragedy as his father left the house and got into the car where his brother and sister waited. As the headlights came on and the car began moving rapidly out of the driveway and down the deserted street, he leaned forward and watched the taillights of the car until at last they disappeared around the corner.

In a few tense moments Peter's father, older brother, and sister had moved silently out of his life. Somehow, as he listened to his mother sobbing in the other room, he knew they would never return.

[Chapter Two]

The heat of the sun beating down on the top of his head caused Peter to awaken early the next morning. He had fallen asleep sitting in the chair beside the window with his head resting on the window sill. Groaning as he straightened himself up, he noticed a large pool of water on the floor under his bare feet. It had seeped through the rotted fibers of the window frame during the night's rainstorm.

Squinting against the bright sunlight pouring into the room through the uncurtained windows, Peter was confused for a moment, uncertain where he was and why. Looking around he noticed his brothers still asleep on the bed. Then, like a tide rushing across a beach, the memories of the night before flooded back. The fight, the screams, his father leaving with David and Sharon, and the long, weary hours alone and frightened in his bedroom. He had waited in terror and despair for his mother to come after his father left. But she never came. Finally sleep rescued him from his nightmare.

Now it was morning. A new day. But where was momma? Why hadn't she come to him like she always did? Peter felt sick at his stomach as a new sense of panic began to grow in him. Maybe his mother was gone too! At that thought the panic swelled into a sudden burst of action as he raced toward the bedroom door, leaving a trail of wet footprints across the dry linoleum floor.

The rustle of his brothers rousing from their sleep

stopped him short of the door. As he turned to look at them, the familiarity of the scene eased his panic. He watched as the two small heads began to appear from under the twisted pile of sheets and blankets. Then the struggle to free themselves from each other and the tangled mass of damp, clinging blankets began.

For a moment Peter felt relieved. He had witnessed this same scene many times before. It was like any other day.

Moving briskly to the bed, Peter grabbed a corner of a blanket and with a sharp tug sent it skimming off the bed and onto the floor. Suddenly exposed and with a gleam of playful delight dancing in their eyes, the two giggling boys bounced across the bed in a tug-of-war in an attempt to be the first to hit the floor. Crashing in a heap of elbows and knees on the floor opposite Peter, they were on their feet in a flash, racing to the closet to get dressed.

Pushing and laughing, they floundered around the small closet for shoes, shirts, shorts, and socks cast carelessly aside the night before. Wishing he could join the fracas, Peter smiled at the two white underweared bottoms knocking around the small cubbyhole.

It was just like every other morning. That helped.

Slowly Peter moved again toward the door. The nagging, uneasy feeling about his mother had returned. "I'm going to see if momma is awake yet," he called out as he closed the bedroom door gently behind him.

The curtains in the rest of the house were still drawn. Peter moved slowly past the gaping door of his brother and sister's bedroom and into the gloom of the hallway. He hoped to hear his mother moving around in another part of the house. But there was only silence. In his parents' bedroom he noticed the bed was still made.

"Momma?" he called out softly.

There was no answer. Frightened again, Peter hesitated as he approached the living room where his parents had been last night. He could hear his heart pounding in his ear.

"Momma?" his tight, squeaky voice called out again. "Momma, where are you?"

With the heavy drapes shut tight, the living room was still very dark. He could see the broken lamp lying in pieces scattered across the floor just inside the room. There were also several beer cans scattered about. But he could not see his mother.

Suddenly a strange rustling sound came from the room. Peter jumped. Fighting the temptation to run, he inched his way cautiously into the room.

"Momma? Is that you, momma?" he whispered.

There was a long moment of uncertain silence before he heard her voice. It sounded hoarse and far away.

"Peter? Is that you, son?"

Sighing deeply with relief, the boy's young body shook uncontrollably as the tension flowed suddenly away.

"Where are you, momma?" he called out.

"On the floor by the couch. Turn on the light, son, and come here."

Peter hurried to do as his mother asked. Fumbling blindly, he found the light switch and flicked it on. The room was suddenly bathed in light from the bare bulb on the ceiling. Then he saw her. She was lying on the floor with her head resting on a pillow propped against the couch. She looked terrible. Her makeup was smeared on her pale face, and the dark rings under her eyes were made darker by the large bruise under her left eye. Her long brown hair lay formless in a tangled mess around her head.

"Momma! Momma! What's the matter, momma?" Peter cried as he hurried to her side.

Her hand felt very cold and lifeless as he picked it up.

"Please, momma, what's the matter?" he pleaded again, peering desperately into her ashen face.

"Peter, please. Talk slowly and softly," she whispered painfully, barely moving her lips to speak.

"All right, momma, I will," the boy promised softly. "But what's the matter, momma? What's wrong with you?"

"Peter. Listen . . . carefully, son. Momma's sick . . .

momma's real sick. You've got to help me, son." The voice became thin and trailed off. For a moment Peter thought she had fallen asleep.

"What do you want me to do, momma?" he asked tearfully as he drew closer to his mother. Once again every muscle in his body was tense as he waited helplessly for her to tell him what he must do to help her. He had never seen his mother like this before.

"Peter, go to the phone. Call Melly. You remember Aunt Melly. When she answers tell her momma is sick and needs help. Ask her if she can come over. Can you do that for momma?"

"Yes, ma'am, I can do that."

"Good, son. Her number is there by the phone." The strain from talking showed on her tired face. Moving to do as his mother asked, he stopped as he saw her trembling hand reach out to take his. "And, son," she said weakly, giving his hand a light squeeze, "don't be frightened. Everything is going to be all right."

There it was! What he so desperately needed to hear. Everything was going to be all right. His mother said so.

Running to the telephone, Peter searched frantically for the phone number she had told him was there; he found it on the top page of the small notepad that she kept under the corner of the phone. Picking up the receiver, he waited to hear the dial tone just as his mother had taught him. Then, he carefully began to dial.

After he dialed the last number, he waited impatiently for the ringing sound that he was supposed to hear. After a series of clicks, it started. He let it ring for what seemed like an awfully long time, as he danced nervously around the small table. Finally he heard a click and the ringing stopped.

"Hello," a sleepy voice mumbled at the other end of the line.

"My momma is sick!" the desperate boy almost shouted into the mouthpiece.

"Who is this?"

"Momma told me to call you. She's sick. She wants you to come over right now. Please help my momma!" the boy begged, beginning to sob. Somehow he had to make her understand.

"Peter? Is that you, Peter?" the woman asked, no longer drowsy.

"Yes, ma'am. Momma is real sick," he repeated the vital message again. "Please come help my momma!"

The woman's voice was suddenly sharp and clear. "All right, Peter. You stay right there with your mother until I can get there. Do you understand?"

"Yes, ma'am."

"Good. I'll be there in a couple of minutes."

The phone clicked again and the voice was replaced by a buzzing sound. Peter hung up the phone and returned to his mother's side. Her fists were clenched tight and her eyes shut.

Just then the last door down the hallway flew open and out stormed Bobby with Jimmy close on his heels. They were dressed and chattering excitedly. As they raced merrily down the hallway, Peter tried to stop them. Seeing their mother lying motionless on the floor, they were startled into silence. Questioning, troubled eyes looked from Peter to their mother and back again.

"We have to be real quiet," Peter explained softly. "Momma is sick and we don't want to wake her up."

Taking hold of their older brother's hands, the two boys sat down with Peter in the large, overstuffed chair. For a long period of anxious silence they watched their mother, as the agonizing minutes ticked away. Then a car pulled up out front and a door slammed.

"That must be her!" Peter whispered anxiously as he ran for the door. He knew that Aunt Melly would know what to do to help his mother.

Dressed in a simple dress, with curlers still in her hair, Aunt Melly moved quickly up the sidewalk to the house. She was a matronly lady with a large body and arms. Her jaw was set in grim determination—expecting the worst—as she marched up the walk, her night slippers slapping at her heels. Running to meet her, Peter grabbed her hand and pulled her into the house.

Without a word the anxious woman entered the living room, her eyes taking in every detail of the scene. Kicking aside an empty beer can, Melly hurried to where Carol lay on the floor. The three boys crowded around her.

"You boys move back now," she commanded after a moment, not taking her eyes off the stricken woman. "I'm going to put your momma to bed where she belongs."

In a matter of moments, she had undressed Carol, put a nightgown on her, and tucked her snugly under the blankets.

Stepping out of the bedroom, Aunt Melly pulled the door shut behind her and went into the kitchen. She sat down at the table and called the boys to her.

With heads down and feet shuffling across thin, worn linoleum, they slowly approached the woman. Wrapping her arms around them, she pulled them close in a hug. For a long moment she held them tightly as though to pour the life and warmth of her own body into theirs.

"Now you boys listen to me," she spoke finally. "Peter, do you remember last winter when you had the mumps?"

"Yes, ma'am."

"Well, you were pretty sick, weren't you?"

"Yes, ma'am. I was real sick!" he exclaimed, remembering how much his throat had hurt.

"But you got well again, didn't you?"

"Yes, ma'am."

"Well, your mother is sick like you were, Peter," she explained, looking at each young agonizing face in turn. "She will have to stay in bed for a few days, but I'm sure she will be well again soon."

"You mean momma has the mumps?" asked Bobby. "I thought mumps was for kids!"

Aunt Melly smiled warmly at the tear-streaked faces gazing up at her.

"Well, no, Bobby, that is not what I mean," she

answered. "Your mother does not have the mumps. But she is sick just the same. But everything is going to be all right. She will be well again soon. I'm sure of it! So you just don't worry now—any of you—do you hear?"

"But she wouldn't talk to us," pointed out Jimmy, still confused and distressed.

"Did Peter talk to you when he was so sick?"

Jimmy thought seriously for a moment before answering.

"No, ma'am."

"Well, see there. You have nothing to worry about, do you?"

"I sure am glad you're here," exclaimed Peter with a deep sigh as he wrapped his arms as far around her neck as they would reach.

"All right now. Let me fix you boys some breakfast and then you can go about your business like always," she stated matter-of-factly as she burst into action in the kitchen.

After a hurried breakfast Peter was sent on his way to school. He felt reassured as he left. Aunt Melly would take care of his mother. Everything was going to be all right after all, even if his father was gone. With his spirits lifted and his mind at ease, Peter turned his thoughts to school.

[Chapter Three]

Peter lost no time in burying himself in the familiar routine of school. He liked school and excelled in most areas. He particularly liked the teacher and worked extra hard to win special attention from her. He learned quickly and was never a discipline problem. But today he was restless. It was hard to concentrate on his work. For some reason he could not sit still and keep quiet. Several times during the morning he disrupted the class with his chatter and idle movement around the room. By lunchtime he had been reprimanded three times. The teacher had even threatened to make him sit in a corner alone if he could not keep from disturbing the other children. That hurt. He could see the confusion and displeasure in her face. As much as he wanted to meet her expectations of him, the distraught boy could not control the nervous movement of his mind and body. It was as if he was being driven by a force beyond his control—a force that seemed to push him in all directions at once.

Peter played hard during the noon recess, even on a full stomach. Hot and sweaty, he had returned reluctantly to his seat in the classroom at the sound of the bell signaling the end of recess. As the teacher read the class a story to settle them down after the lunch break, Peter laid his head on his arms in front of him and was soon fast asleep.

Shaking him gently, the teacher awoke him a few minutes later. Although it was hard to open his eyelids and his mind was slow to grasp what was happening, Peter recognized the voice of his teacher calling to him. Pulling himself forcefully out of the heavy grasp of sleep toward her voice, he was able at last to focus his eyes on her face.

"Yes, ma'am?" he mumbled.

"Peter, what in the world is the matter with you today? This isn't like you," she went on without waiting for an answer. "You are being a very naughty young man! Is there something wrong?"

"No, ma'am," Peter answered, sitting up straight in the chair and trying to look alert.

"Are you ill?" she asked as she put her hand to his forehead. "You don't feel like you are running a temperature. Don't you feel well, Peter?"

Suddenly Peter began to cry hysterically. Deeply concerned the teacher knelt beside his chair and held him close for a moment, rocking gently side to side. Being so close to her had a calming effect upon the boy. After awhile his crying began to diminish.

"My goodness, Peter, can you tell me what's wrong?" she whispered softly in his ear.

"I don't know," he gulped between sobs.

"Peter, can you tell me why you are crying?" she tried once more as she lifted his head off her shoulder and looked into his face.

"Because I don't feel good," he blurted out between sobs.

"Well, why don't you feel good?" her voice was soft and maternal.

"Because I'm a bad boy."

"Oh, Peter, for heaven's sake! You're not a bad boy," she tried to reassure him. "OK, so we've had a bad day. Everybody has a bad day once in awhile. It's all right. Now stop crying and I'll tell you what we can do." She waited a minute while open palms wiped away tears from puffy red eyes. "That's better. Now, let's pretend that none of this has happened. Let's start all over right now with this day, just like it is morning. How does that sound?"

"OK," Peter mumbled, not wanting her to move away from him.

"Good! Let's do that!"

Suddenly she was on her feet and once again giving her attention to the class, leaving Peter to renewed depression. He wanted so much to please her, but he felt so tired. And sleepy. All he wanted was for someone to rock him to sleep.

The afternoon ticked relentlessly away. Peter's behavior was just the opposite of what it had been that morning. He sat passively and quietly in his chair, participating in the class activities only when called upon. All his feeling had poured out of him with his tears, leaving behind an emptiness heavy with its own nothingness. There was no pain. Only a weight that dragged him deeper and deeper into himself.

Mercifully three o'clock finally arrived. Now he could be alone. He trailed the other children out of the classroom, but hid in the bathroom hoping his usual walking companions would go on without him. Sitting on the edge of the toilet, he slouched forward with his head almost resting on his knees. The tremendous fatigue he felt made even the slightest movement a difficult one.

Drifting somewhere within his own thinking, the troubled boy noticed nothing around him: not the fly buzzing persistently around his head, nor the pungent fragrance of restroom deodorant, nor the constant drip of water in the urinal along the length of opposite wall. Nor did he notice the passing of time as deep shadows began moving resolutely across the tiled floor toward him.

The unrelenting need to urinate made Peter aware again of where he was and why. Standing up he moved limply to the urinal and began relieving himself absentmindedly, staring blindly into the basin. Not caring about the wet spots on the legs of his pants, Peter left the restroom and methodically began his lonely walk home.

The air felt heavy and moist as he moved across the empty playground to the street. Deciding in favor of a shortcut his parents had warned him not to take, Peter began making his way slowly through the maze of back alleys littered with garbage, cut shrubbery, and other human unwantables toward his home on Oak Street.

Tall dark clouds, boiling with a mounting fury all their own, were forming to the southwest, threatening to drench the small western town in another deluge like that of the night before. Pausing to rest for a moment on the top of a garbage can, Peter watched as a jagged bolt of lightning struck wickedly at some object on the ground far away. A moment later he heard the deep rumble of thunder.

Becoming aware of his aloneness in the alley, he had a deep yearning to be held in his mother's arms, and that stirred him to action once more. With a sense of urgency he clambered off the top of the garbage can and quickly continued his journey home. Fighting hard against the lump swelling in his throat, he anxiously began to hurry his steps until, all else forgotten, he was running headlong down the narrow alleys with all the speed his small legs could generate. He had to jump, dodge, and weave to avoid objects in his path.

"Please be well, momma!" he cried to himself as he raced on. Breathing heavily, and with legs weak from the strain, Peter at last shot out of a back alley into the middle of Oak Street. Towering maple trees lined both sides, spreading a full multicolored canopy of leaves low across its width. Here and there small shafts of late afternoon sunlight spilled onto the lush green lawns that blended one into the other along the sidewalks. It was a pretty street, his mother had observed many times during their evening walks through the neighborhood, despite the small, unpainted houses with their broken windows and sagging roofs. With the storm brewing in the distance, Oak Street was a scene of peace about to be shattered.

Turning to a sidewalk, Peter raced down its length, ignoring the friendly wave of the corner grocery store owner. On any other day he would have stopped for a few minutes to stare longingly into the candy case positioned strategically near the window.

For a moment Peter felt reassured as the surroundings became more and more familiar the closer he got to his home. But then, still two blocks away, he saw the ambulance backed into the driveway, its red lights flashing and back doors gaping wide.

The curious neighbors standing in a small group on the lawn in front of the house and murmuring among themselves did not notice the boy come up behind the large maple tree that dominated the front yard. Quietly he stood there, watching.

Soon two men in white shirts with red cross patches on their sleeves carried his mother out of the house on a bed with wheels. Lifting the bed carefully off the porch, they rolled his mother to the rear of the ambulance.

Peter watched her face as she moved past him. Her eyes were closed tightly and she looked as she had that morning. Desperately he wanted to run to her, to make her wake up, and make them take her back into the house. But he didn't. Instead, he bit hard on already swelling knuckles and watched as the two men lifted her into the rear of the ambulance and closed the doors.

Wrapping his arms around the trunk of the tree that hid

him from the other people standing in the yard, Peter sank to the ground on his knees and watched the ambulance carry his mother away from him down the same street he had seen his father's car disappear the night before. She was gone. Just like his father, his mother was gone.

With his face pressed hard against the tree trunk, Peter stared with dry but aching eyes at the spot down the street where she had gone. Soon the neighbors dispersed to their own homes.

Long after they were gone the boy picked himself up and moved toward the front door of the house, which was still propped open by a chair. Once inside he moved straight for his parents' bedroom, the last place she had been when he left her that morning. Fixing his eyes on the bed, the boy saw nothing else. But he saw the bed. Every inch of it. Every wrinkle, every crease, every spot on the sheets. Looking carefully he could still see the shape of her head on the pillow.

It was nearly dark when Aunt Melly finally found him standing like a statue frozen in its place, staring with empty eyes at where his mother had been. Several times she called to the boy, but received no response. He made no sound, no movement.

Taking his lifeless hand in her strong one, she pulled the boy away from the bed and through the door into the world waiting outside. He didn't resist. He didn't care.

[PART II]
The Foster Homes

* * * *

Peter was barely six years old when his biological family was torn apart by divorce. Though a period of marital separation occurred before the divorce was finalized, as far as Peter was concerned it all happened within the course of one day.

Divorce can be a traumatic experience for children under the most amiable conditions. Fear of losing one or both parents and the uncertainty of having to face alone a frightening future are major concerns. Children are acutely aware of their total dependence upon their parents for the necessities of life, not to mention the love and nurturing they so desperately need. Threatened or actual loss of the family can have tragic consequences for the children, particularly if there is not a nurturing caregiver present to help the children interpret the events. Left to their own imaginations, children tend not only to fantasize the worst, but to fasten blame for the family troubles upon themselves. They assume that they are the cause of the conflict precipitating the family breakup.

Such was the case with Peter. During a period of twenty-four hours, his greatest fears were realized. He watched his father leave the family, taking his older brother and sister with him. He watched his mother as she was carried away from him in an ambulance. Suddenly he was alone in an empty house. Understanding none of it, Peter rationalized all of it—blaming himself.

**By the time the State Child Welfare Department
intervened on his behalf, Peter had reacted to his
overpowering feelings of loss, guilt, and personal helplessness by withdrawing into a private world of fantasy.
The efforts made by the welfare department to provide
him a safe home in which to live in the days, months, and
years to follow, in the long run only hurt him more. What
he needed most they were unprepared to give him.**

[Chapter Four]

With his Stetson pushed far back on his head, the tall
deputy sheriff knelt painfully on the uncarpeted floor.
Bending as far forward as possible, his chin inches off the
floor, he strained to see the boy through the darkness under
the bed. The contrasting glare of late afternoon August
sunlight which filled the room made his eyes hurt as they
adjusted to the darkness. Squinting hard, he could see the
boy's shape in the shadows around him.

"Now, Peter, you come on out of there!" the deputy's
weary voice commanded. Seeing no response from the
shadows, the man sighed deeply and tried once more. "Son,
listen to me. I'm not going to hurt you. Why don't you just
come on out of there like a good boy? There's nothing to be
afraid of. Come on out now. Here, I'll give you a hand," he
pleaded, reaching a short distance under the bed.

Peter lay coiled in a knot in the furthest corner away
from the man. His legs were drawn up tightly under his
chin, ready to lash out if the hand should draw too close.
With his back pressed firmly against the base of the wall,
his hands clung tenaciously to the rusty bedsprings just
above his head. This time he was going to fight back!

Ignoring the pleas, the determined boy watched the
sweat drip from the tired, leathery face peering at him only
a few short feet away. Not a twitch of an eye nor the

movement of a facial muscle escaped his notice. He particularly watched the eyes, the tightening and loosening of the muscles around them as they changed from cold hues to warm, soft colors and back again. He carefully measured every expression, every movement of that face, knowing from experience with many strangers that a person's intentions would show there first. Survival meant being able to predict a stranger's intentions before they became action so as not to be caught off guard.

As the minutes ticked away, another face, much younger, would occasionally join that of the deputy's peering intently into the darkness trying to see Peter. Together they made a bizarre picture of frustrated adults turned upside down.

Peter remembered that face. He had seen it on several previous occasions. And each time he had grown to hate it more. That was Mr. White, the man from the State Child Welfare Department.

Peter had been playing in the front yard when the sheriff's patrol car had pulled to the curb and stopped in front of their house. At first he had been curious, having never been so close to a real patrol car. But as soon as the door on the passenger side opened and Mr. White stepped out, Peter knew exactly why the patrol car had stopped at their house. Just like the other times, Mr. White had come to take him away from his mother.

Dashing madly into the house and past his mother, Peter had taken refuge under the bed. It was going to be different this time. He was older now, and stronger. He was not going to let them take him away like before. This time he was going to fight back!

How he hated that face! Setting his jaw in ferocious determination, the boy tensed the muscles in his arms and legs, and waited.

Peter was eight now. The two and a half years since his mother had been taken in the ambulance to the mental hospital had been tough, painful ones. He had not seen his father since that dreadful night so long ago. Nor had he heard from his older brother and sister. How desperately he had missed them all at first. Particularly his mother and sister, the two people he loved most in all the world. They were the two most familiar to him, having always been there in times of need or want to nurture and protect him in his infancy.

Immediately following the breakup of his family, Aunt Melly had taken the three boys into her home for several weeks while the State Child Welfare Department arranged state custody and temporary foster homes. Peter never asked why his father did not come for them. The thought never occurred to him. Having been left behind the night his father left, he assumed, at a level that precedes cognition, that he and his younger brothers were not wanted.

Peter could remember very little of those first few days. The shock of sudden, compounded loss in so short a period of time dulled his senses to what was happening about him. Times, places, and faces blended together into a dream filled with pain, but no content. Nothing seemed real anymore. What used to be his father became a pair of taillights disappearing around a corner. His brother and sister became anxious voices crying in the dark. And where his mother had been was now left only an image on an empty bed. Each had been replaced by fantasy. Like a sea anemone touched by a foreign object, Peter had withdrawn into himself, behind a protective shield of passive indifference to all about him; a private world where he could survive, alone, as he attempted to adjust and understand. Only the pain remained the same. Survival meant controlling the pain. To do this, his untrained mind sought to deny the cause in a headlong flight into fantasy. The fear he felt was for anything that threatened the security of his fantasies.

For hours on end the troubled boy would sit alone, mute, subdued, and withdrawn. He would make no effort to interact with his environment except for his younger brothers. They became his only real link to the world around him. Now that both their parents were gone, Peter felt a special responsibility to protect and care for them. Only they, with their endless wants, needs, and chatter, could get a response from him. They became his one anchor to reality.

After several days of heartbreaking attempts to stir the boy into a renewed interest in life, Aunt Melly had given up in despair. Deeply saddened, she had resigned herself to providing for his physical care only.

As time went by, Peter became more and more interested in his brothers, spending more time each day with them. He grew possessive and protective of them, clinging tenaciously to them as the only remnants of his family. Within days his attachment to them deepened into a lifetime commitment to their welfare. They became inseparable. Any feelings he had left were directed toward them. They became the most important people in his life.

Then came the day the welfare workers arrived to take the boys to the foster homes arranged for them. Without hesitation or resistance Peter had gone with Mr. White, not knowing that he was being separated from his brothers, because they had been placed in separate homes.

It was not until the car began pulling away from the curb that Peter realized what was happening. Like an animal caged for the first time, he was suddenly on all fours searching out his brothers through the rear window of the car. Clawing desperately, he tore at the door, trying to get out. When the door would not budge he struggled madly across the vinyl seat to the other door, jerking wildly at the handle. In a panic he sought another escape. Just as he started over the back of the front seat, a large hand closed around his neck, forcing him abruptly back onto the rear seat. With arms and legs flailing, he fought to free himself from the hand gripping his neck. With teeth gnashing at the arm beside his head, Peter suddenly went limp as he was stunned by the sting of a palm slapped across the side of his face.

"Now you listen to me, young man," screeched the welfare worker through gritted teeth, still firmly gripping the boy's neck. "Don't you ever try that little stunt again or I'll knock the crap out of you. Do you hear me, boy?"

Unable to speak because of the hand's iron grip on his neck, Peter fastened his eyes on a pore in the man's nose only an inch from his own and struggled for a deep breath of air. For the first time in his life there were no tears to ease the pain. Coupled with his own helplessness, the pain in his face and neck only provided fuel for a beginning rage smoldering somewhere deep inside him. With eyes blazing fear and anger, the troubled boy finally had a target for all the hostility that lay buried in the shallow grave of his mind.

"Now you settle down back there and don't give me any more trouble the rest of the way," the welfare worker commanded, releasing his grip slowly. Peter huddled out of sight in the corner behind the driver's seat as the car began to move down the street once again.

Several hours later Peter found himself all alone in a strange house with strange people. It was then, while sitting on the couch in the living room staring at the faces staring at him, that he made up his mind to do whatever was necessary to find his sister and brothers. He would escape. Somehow he would find a way to escape and find them. Or die trying.

Like a person obsessed, Peter replaced his fantasies with purpose. Now he spent much of his time looking, watching, and thinking; he plotted his escape from this family. The depression that had lingered with him for so long now turned to sullenness. Though never openly hostile toward the foster family, Peter kept the low-grade rage simmering just below the surface—his attitude cold and aloof from them. In his mind they represented only a barrier which had to be overcome in order to find his brothers. To that end he sought ways to manipulate them into complacency, hoping their backs would turn just long enough for him to escape.

But before he could make his move, Mr. White took him to another foster home. Unable to reach the boy with their care and concern, and frightened by his sullen, unpredictable behavior, the family had requested that he be removed from their home.

So began the progression of foster homes for Peter, usually at two- or three-month intervals. He lived in several different foster homes during the two-year period following the breakup of his family. At first he did not care. Frustrated in his obsession to escape one home, he had renewed hope and opportunity with each one.

After awhile Peter adjusted somewhat to the absence of his baby brothers. Though he lived for the day of reunion with them and his sister, his driving obsession became tempered with yet another drive—the need to be touched and held. Each new family came to mean more than just another opportunity to escape; each came to represent a new start, another chance to be loved, wanted, and accepted. Torn between his obsessive need to escape and his need for physical affection, Peter would be drawn slowly out of his shell, usually just long enough to meet his most pressing need and then hastily retreat into sullenness. As his efforts were rewarded, his trust of the family members and environment would grow until he would take more risks, opening up more often and for longer periods of time in his search for human warmth and acceptance. He was desperate.

Peter now lived daily in the midst of desperation—desperate to escape and desperate to survive. His cautious reaching out to his foster family was a desperate attempt to be loved and wanted.

But then, just when he would begin to feel reasonably secure in his new home with his new family, the long arm of Mr. White and the State Child Welfare Department would reach deep into his life, suddenly yanking him out of his environment by the roots, and transplant him somewhere else. Always suddenly, always unexpectedly. Another town perhaps, another home, another family, another scar.

Each move became more painful than the last because each convinced the boy that no one loved him or wanted him. As a result, each new family found it harder than the last to draw him even briefly out of his shell. It was as though he no longer cared enough to take the risk and try. He seemed perfectly content to spend all his time alone and silent.

Concerned about his emotional condition, the State Child Welfare Department thought a brief visit with his younger brothers might bring Peter out of his shell. A weekend picnic was arranged in a state park on the outskirts of town.

At first the social service guardians of the boys watched them closely with an eye for the unexpected. They did not know how Peter would react to seeing his brothers again. Although he was never more than a few feet from the adults, Peter was laughing and chattering with his brothers; the reunion seemed to have accomplished its purpose. After nearly an hour without incident, the social workers tired of their surveillance and became more interested in each other. Intent upon their conversation they failed to notice the boys drifting further and further away, ever closer to the small, shallow stream that separated the park grounds from the thickly wooded forest pressing in on the other side.

Soon the boys were gone. With a quick glance over his shoulder at the lounging social workers, Peter hurried his brothers across the stream and headlong into the woods. A half hour passed before their absence was noted.

With the sun dipping ever closer to the horizon, a search party of forty men stretched the half mile length of the stream bordering the park and began their probe of the thickly wooded area. Advancing slowly straight ahead, each man penetrated deeper and deeper into the darkening woods.

As the last rays of sunlight vanished into twilight, the boys had not been found. Using flashlights the men searched all night. Just as the sun began frosting the tops of the trees early the next morning, a call from a police cruiser came over the radio that three small boys matching the description of Peter and his brothers had been picked up trying to hitchhike along a deserted stretch of highway four miles north of the search site.

When asked later where he and his brothers were going, Peter had answered "Home."

While his brothers were returned immediately to their foster homes, Peter was detained several days for observation in a child detention center. Eventually he was returned to his foster home.

Having failed in his attempted escape with his brothers, Peter became increasingly more hostile and destructive. In the days that followed nothing material was safe in his presence as he acted out his rage on the world about him. The progression of foster homes continued.

Just as the angry young man was about to be placed as an incorrigible into one of the state's correction facilities for delinquent boys, his mother petitioned the state for a return of custody to her. She was working, and she was sure that she could manage the boys and their life together.

That was the happiest day of Peter's young life. All three boys were back with their mother. How they all laughed and played together! It was almost like he remembered. Walks in the neighborhood, church on Sunday mornings, his mother busy in the kitchen singing softly to herself, bedtime stories, and lots of hugs. Peter's frozen heart thawed quickly by the warmth of her presence, and once again he felt secure in their life together. He became sure that nothing would ever tear them apart again.

But that was six months ago. Now Mr. White from the State Child Welfare Department was back. This time to take the boys away for good.

Somehow Peter knew this as he clung with all his might to the rusty bedsprings under the bed. How he hated that face staring at him!

"Come on, Peter, be a big boy now," coaxed the welfare worker as he reached out slowly for the boy's foot. Within inches of its target, the foot shot out with all the force of young muscled legs, smashing the outstretched hand hard into the ragged bedsprings. The pain of small pieces of flesh being torn from the back of his hand caused the welfare worker to withdraw it hurriedly.

"Damn!" he exclaimed, as a small trickle of blood moved across the back of his hand. Feeling the deputy's eyes on him, he tried to explain. "Well dammit, John, he kicked me!"

"What did you expect? The kid is scared to death," the deputy responded, unmoved. " Here, let me take a look at that hand."

"Naw, it's all right," he answered sullenly, dabbing gently at the several small wounds with his handkerchief.

"Suit yourself."

With a scowl creasing his forehead, the deputy returned his attention to getting the stubborn boy out from under the bed without scaring or hurting him. After a long thoughtful moment he turned reluctantly to the social worker.

"Got any fresh ideas?"

"No, I guess I don't," he answered, his voice showing his frustration. "He's sure not going to come out of there on his own. That's obvious. I think we are just going to have to force him out. I don't see any other way."

"You care to reach under there and try to grab that foot again?" the deputy asked with a hint of a smile playing at the corners of his mouth.

Turning red, the welfare worker got up and moved to the window. With his back to the room he stared intently at something outside.

"Well, let me talk to his mother one more time," the deputy said finally in the midst of a deep sigh. Getting up, he moved to the front porch of the house. His boots scraped against the grit on the surface as he walked slowly across the narrow length of the porch and sat down beside the thin, frail woman sitting motionless in the swing.

"Miz Cunningham?" he began. "Your boy has crawled under the bed in the corner over there and won't come out. Now, ma'am, you know we have to get him out of there. Could you please help us get him to come out, please, ma'am?"

Staring blindly into the empty space around her, the woman seemed deaf to the man's words. She made no response. The deputy tried again.

"Miz Cunningham, please. We've got to get the boy out of there one way or another. You know that. Please don't make us have to drag him out like some kind of animal. We don't want to hurt the boy, ma'am."

Turning her head slowly, the woman looked long and hard at the older man sitting uncomfortably beside her. After a moment she spoke.

"Offer him a chocolate milkshake," her voice was tired and unemotional. "His father could get him to do anything for a chocolate milkshake."

"A chocolate milkshake?" the man responded incredulously. The idea blossomed in his mind. "Now that's an idea! We haven't tried that yet. Yes, yes that just might do the trick."

In a flurry of motion the deputy left her sitting alone once again in the swing and hurried back into the bedroom. Ignoring the curious look of the welfare worker, he dropped purposively to his knees once again beside the bed. After a moment for his eyes to adjust, he could see the boy still cowering in the corner. The deputy began to speak to the boy like he might to his own son.

"Peter, listen to me, son. Have you ever ridden in a patrol car? A real patrol car with flashing lights and the siren going full blast?"

Waiting for this to sink in, he noticed the welfare worker approaching the bed. Waving him away cautiously, the deputy strained to see some movement under the bed. There was none.

"Peter?"

There was no answer.

"Would you like to ride in a real patrol car, Peter? Sitting in the front seat where you can see everything that's going on? Would you like that, Peter?"

Still there was no response.

"I'll tell you what I'm going to do, Peter, just for you. I'm going to give you and your brothers a free ride in my patrol car. And I will even let you turn on the siren all by yourself. Would you like that, son? You know what else? I'll just bet that none of your friends have ever ridden in a real patrol car with a real deputy sheriff, have they, son? Imagine what your friends will say when they find out you have! How does that sound to you, Peter?"

Reluctantly and suspiciously Peter began to be interested. Sensing the boy's moment of weakness, the deputy decided to play his ace.

"And you know what else, Peter? I will even buy you a chocolate milkshake to boot! What do you think about that?"

The mention of a chocolate milkshake sent a flood of old, warm feelings sweeping through the boy, special feelings between a boy and his father during a time long past, but well remembered. Suddenly Peter wanted a chocolate milkshake very badly.

"Really?"

"Really, son."

"Cross your heart and hope to die?"

"Cross my heart and hope to die."

"No King's X's?"

"No King's X's."

Peter weighed the offer for a moment.

"Can I have one all for myself?"

"Yes, son, you can have a great big one all for yourself."

Distracted from his reason for being under the bed in the first place, Peter gave in. Using short, snakelike movements of his body, he wiggled and squirmed his way out from under the bed.

"Well, I'll be damned!" exclaimed the welfare worker as the deputy grabbed one of Peter's arms and he the other. "If that wasn't a piece of slick . . . ." He was silenced by a glare from the deputy.

With a man on each side of him, Peter was marched out of the house, across the porch in front of his mother, down the cracked sidewalk, and seated firmly in the backseat of the patrol car. His younger brothers were already there.

As the back door of the car slammed shut, Peter noticed that there were no doorhandles on the back doors. He also noticed that there was a metal screen separating the front seat from the back.

The realization of what he had done struck him like a blow. He had let them take him away from his mother again. And now he was trapped! Just like before.

Hating himself bitterly for letting it happen, Peter rested his head on the window glass beside him. As the patrol car pulled slowly away from the curb and began its winding journey into another world, he watched his mother still sitting motionless in the swing on the porch. Only he saw her head suddenly drop into her lap as her thin body was wracked with vicious sobs of grief. Although he had no idea why he was being taken away from his mother this time, he knew then that he would never live with his mother again.

The bloodcurdling scream that began in his mind found no outlet through his mouth, but continued long after his mother was lost from sight.

[Chapter Five]

The sheriff's patrol car made its way along the winding country road, moving deeper into the countryside. Huddled in a corner of the backseat, Peter watched absentmindedly as the thickly wooded landscape moved past, broken occasionally by an open meadow of tall grass splashed with patches of colorful late summer wildflowers. His mind would jump with curiosity at the occasional sight of cattle grazing aimlessly in one of the many pastures along the way, or at the cowboys astraddle their thundering horses herding reluctant cattle across the road in front of them. Despite all that he had been through in his short life, Peter still saw the world around him through the excited eyes of a child as a place of mystery and adventure. It was like a fairy tale unfolding before his very eyes, a story of cowboys and Indians, of horses and cattle and dogs, of wagon trains, campfires, and countless adventures with outlaws and rustlers.

The fantasy played on in his imagination as the minutes passed from one to the next. The shadows of trees began to lengthen across the road, replacing more and more of the sparkling sunlight reflecting off the glistening gravel.

Peter had no idea where he and his brothers were being taken. Having resigned himself to once again being placed in a foster home, he was relieved that he had not been separated from his brothers this time. He somehow felt safer with the metal screen protecting them from the two men in the front seat. At least they could not reach through the screen and take his brothers away too.

Although the deputy had made a couple of attempts to talk with him, Peter had shown no interest, and the deputy had given up. The welfare worker ignored him entirely. No mention was made of sirens, patrol cars, or chocolate milkshakes.

Although the trip from his mother's house to the foster farm took less than three hours by the clock, it took much longer than that by any other measurement. It had taken Peter six years of living with his mother and two years without her to arrive at this moment in his life. A lifetime of coming and going that came and went. Now, it was the end of the line. Only he and his younger brothers were left. The door to the only world he knew and wanted was closing behind him forever, to be sealed permanently. There would be no returning to his mother this time. Never again would he live with his mother or family. They were a part of his life soon to become memories; memories tinged with yearning at first, but later only curiosity. Only his younger brothers would accompany him on his quest for adulthood and freedom. Although Peter somehow knew all this, he had no way of knowing that he and his brothers had been put up for adoption. They were being taken to a foster home where they would stay only until the adoptions could be arranged.

Plummeting deeper and deeper into the uncertainties of a world without his family, Peter felt no fear. He had been in so many foster homes already that he knew basically what to expect. Everything would be the same as the other times. Only the names and faces would be different. And those did not matter.

What he felt most was an intense bitterness toward himself for giving in to the deputy and allowing himself to be taken away without a fight. The consequences of his moment of weakness took a heavy toll on the boy. As he moved further and further away from home, he became more and more convinced that it was all his fault. It would have never happened if not for his weakness. The pleasure of chocolate milkshakes melted into a grotesque abhorrence. What had drawn him closer to his father and made him feel special had driven him a lifetime away from his mother and made him feel rotten. He was bad. He was sure of it. He deserved to be hurt and punished. It was all his fault. And all because of a chocolate milkshake. He would be an adult before he would touch a chocolate milkshake again without the urge to throw up.

As much as Peter hated himself, he despised the two men sitting in the front seat of the car even more. They represented a power and authority far greater than his own; a power so great they could do anything they wanted with him, even take him away from his mother. They were adults. That was all it took. They had all the power and there was nothing in the world he could do about it—at least, not yet.

"That's it!" exclaimed the deputy sheriff as the patrol car topped a hill and began its descent into a small valley.

The shattering of the drowsy silence in the car caught Peter's attention. Inching forward in the seat, he surveyed the scene unfolding before his eyes.

The valley was rimmed by heavily wooded hills on every side. Large granite boulders, evidence of a violent and fiery past, protruded from the red clay dirt everywhere except those areas which had been cleared for planting and pasture over the years. The gravel road split the valley into halves. On the right was a large open pasture with patches of trees clustered about to provide shade for the livestock during the hottest periods of the long summer days. In the middle of the pasture was a small pond, its water shimmering in the late afternoon sun. Peter wondered at the several cattle standing half submerged in the pond. Several other cattle and a couple of horses were grazing on the short cropped grass nearby. A barbed wire fence lined the meadow just at the point where the openness of the meadow ended and the thickly wooded forest began.

To the left of the road was a small farmhouse, its blue shingled roof standing out against the sea of green around it. A short distance beyond the house stood a large barn, its tin roof rusty from years of climactic changes. Split rail fences protected the yard from straying livestock. The rest of the farm was fenced in barbed wire, except for the wooden corrals on two sides of the barn. In the middle of the barnyard stood an old smokehouse with chinks of plaster missing between several logs. Directly behind the barn was the chickenhouse, a scene of lazy activity as poultry pecked listlessly with random abandonment. The farm sat on the edge of a pasture as large as the one on the opposite side of the road. The young boy's eyes were drawn magnetically to the small river that meandered its way along the furthest reaches of the pasture until it disappeared in a thick growth of forest.

Peter's fascination with the animals increased as they appeared to grow larger the closer the car moved to the front entrance to the farm, until at last the boy's nose was flattened against the side window glass as he stared curiously at the animals now only a few feet away. They were larger than he had thought they would be. He had seen farm animals before only from a distance. Despite his many homes, none had been a real farm.

"This is the end of the line, boys," the welfare worker said as the car pulled off the gravel road and came to a stop in front of the farmhouse. "This is your new home."

Peter had been so engrossed in the scene around him that he had forgotten momentarily the presence of the two men in the front seat. His concentration shattered by the voice, Peter crashed forcefully into the corner of the seat, wrapping his arms tightly around his knees pulled up under his chin. For a moment his eyes blazed defiantly, but then as quickly returned to their cold, empty stare as the welfare worker turned suddenly to look at him.

Jimmy and Bobby had slept during most of the trip. The sudden, quiet stillness roused them from their long naps. Then they saw the dogs racing to meet the car. Brightened with smiles, the eager boys began clamoring to be set free. The deputy sheriff opened the back door of the car and laughed as the two boys tumbled in a heap at his feet.

"Well, now, you boys just come right on out of there," he invited. "This is your new home."

The younger boys had hardly regained their footing before they were buried in a pile of friendly, eager dogs. Laughing and chattering excitedly, they raced away from the car with the dogs in hot pursuit of their new playmates.

Peter remained huddled alone in the backseat as the deputy sheriff and welfare worker moved stiffly toward the house, trying to stretch their legs as they walked. Suddenly his eyes were drawn to yet another dog lingering hesitantly in the front yard. He was smaller than the others and seemed to have less hair. For a long moment Peter watched him standing alone in the yard, eyeing the car suspiciously, his head and tongue drooping from the heat. Then the dog began moving slowly toward the car only to stop as his attention was drawn toward the others romping wildly about the yard. Just as he seemed ready to break away to join the others, his eyes returned to the car as though he knew there was another boy left there.

The deputy sheriff and welfare worker made their way along the beaten path to the front door of the farmhouse. As they drew near the front porch, the screen door suddenly burst open and out poured Mrs. Jones.

"Howdy, y'all!" she exclaimed, stepping lightly off the porch and into the yard. "Been expectin' you boys all day."

"Sorry, ma'am. We had a little trouble getting away," the deputy explained. "Hope we didn't inconvenience you much."

"Not a bit. I just stayed close by the house so's I could hear the car drive up."

"Well, ma'am, I'm glad to hear that," the deputy continued. "Ma'am, I'm deputy John McCullum and this here's Steve White," he explained, pointing in the general direction of the welfare worker beside him. "He's with the State Welfare Office in the city."

"I'm pleased to make both your acquaintances," the woman smiled warmly. "Come on up here on the porch out of that sun while I fetch us some lemonade."

Unable to do anything else, the men were herded onto the front porch and into the swing suspended from a large beam in the roof. In moments the woman reappeared on the porch extending wet, dripping mason quart jars full of ice cold lemonade.

The conversation between the welfare worker and Mrs. Jones lasted only about ten minutes. She listened patiently while watching the boys playing in the yard.

"Do you have any questions I can answer for you now before we leave?" he concluded, looking suggestively at the deputy stretched out comfortably in the swing.

"No, Mr. White, I reckon not. We've had foster children before. None of this is new to us."

"Well, that's fine," exclaimed the welfare worker. "Guess that about does it, John. I'll get the kids' things out of the car and we can head for home and supper."

Mr. White left the swing and headed for the car. He could

see Peter still sitting in the corner of the seat, away from the open door, staring absentmindedly at something in the yard.

"Come on out of there, Peter!" he commanded as he waited by the door. Seeing no response to his command, he leaned far into the backseat to grab the boy's arm and jerk him forcefully across the seat to the open door. "You get your butt out of this car, boy! Now!"

Ignoring the pain in his arm, Peter obeyed. Entering the front yard, he approached slowly toward the dog now intently watching his every move. Before reaching the dog, Peter sat down in the grass and crossed his legs in front of him. For long moments animal and boy stared silently at each other. The dog rose to its feet and, with eyes riveted to those of the boy, moved half a distance closer before once again settling himself in the grass. After a while longer the dog lowered his head and inched his way in a low crouch closer to the boy, until at last he stood expectantly in front of him. Reaching out slowly, Peter began stroking the dog's head. At the first gentle touch, dog and tail came alive. With tail wagging wildly, the dog climbed eagerly into Peter's lap and began licking his face. The dog's tongue felt hot and wet, but Peter did not mind. It somehow felt good. The gentleness of it sent a warm tingle throughout his body. It was almost like being kissed on the cheek by his mother.

Having placed the boys' baggage on the front porch, the two men started toward the car. Before their final good-bye could be spoken, a booming laughing voice greeted them from the side of the house.

"Howdy do! Sorry I wasn't here to meet you boys. Been tendin' to some chores."

A tall, lanky man dressed in work boots, denims, and straw hat came striding around the corner of the house toward them.

"This here's my husband," explained the woman.

"Don't apologize, Mr. Jones. We understand," said the welfare worker. "We have told your wife everything you need to know about the boys. Maybe she can fill you in on the details."

"I reckon she can," the middle-aged farmer agreed. "Them's our new boys, huh?"

"Yes, sir, those are your new boys."

"Fine lookin' bunch. Little skinny maybe. Reckon you can fatten them up a little?" he asked, turning to his wife.

"Oh, I suspect I can," she answered with a smile.

"They're fine boys, Mr. Jones," declared the welfare worker. "The oldest one over there might give you a little trouble. But you just let me know if he tries anything."

"A little feller like that cause trouble? Why, you just don't worry about them boys. They'll do just fine!"

After a moment more of neighborly chatter, the two men climbed into the car and disappeared in a cloud of dust in the direction they had come.

Left alone with their new family, the couple sat in the swing on the porch watching the boys playing in the front yard. Occasionally their heads would touch as they talked quietly. After a few minutes Mr. Jones eased himself out of the swing and walked toward the barn.

Mrs. Jones remained seated in the swing. She was watching Peter. The other two boys had disappeared around the corner of the house, headed for parts unknown with a pack of dogs nipping playfully at their heels. Peter was still sitting alone in the yard. The dog was now cradled in his lap. As the last bit of bright red sun dipped below the horizon behind him, Mrs. Jones watched as the boy wrapped his small arms around the dog's neck and hugged the animal close. She saw him rest his cheek on the top of the dog's head as he began rocking gently back and forth.

What she did not see was what Peter hid from her, especially the tiny tears sliding down the length of his nose and dropping off into the dry, light fur of the animal, there to be absorbed and exist no more. In a small voice he knew she would not hear, Peter sang softly to himself and the animal.

"Jesus loves me! this I know. . . ."

It was a song his mother had taught him. When he was a child. A long time ago.

[Chapter Six]

Morning comes early on a farm. The day after the arrival was no exception. Peter was awakened long before the others by the relentless announcements of an anxious rooster. The darkness still in the house told him that it was not yet time to get up. He was sure no one else was up. The house was too quiet. Peter slipped lightly out from under the covers and off the bed, trying hard not to awaken his brothers, and began dressing hurriedly. Despite his fear of the strange, unfamiliar darkness around him, the boy knew that he could not go back to sleep, no matter how hard he tried. There was only one thought on his mind—the dog. Like a drowning swimmer grasping frantically after a drifting log, Peter felt driven to find the dog, now. His fear was to awaken into the third act of a different play with a different script, props, and characters. And the dog would not be one of them. Desperately he needed to awaken into the same scene he had gone to sleep in the night before. He needed the dog, to see it, to touch it, to hold it in his lap as he had the day before, to continue believing that it was real and loved him as much as he loved it, to feel the warmth of its fur pressed softly against his face. Even more, Peter needed desperately to know the dog was still there.

Awakening to that single thought, Peter knew this was his chance. Moving faster, the boy walked quickly down the hallway, into the kitchen, and silently out the unlocked back screen door into the yard.

"Here, boy! Come here, boy!" he called out anxiously as he looked around the corner of the house. Suddenly, out of nowhere, the animal appeared beside him, its tail wagging fiercely. Like a weight lifter whose legs give out under too much weight, Peter dropped to his knees and fell upon the dog's neck with quiet sobs of relief.

"You're still here, aren't you, boy? You didn't go away, did you? No! What a good doggie. You wouldn't leave me, would you?"

Pulling the dog into his lap and talking softly to him, Peter settled himself on the grass with his back to the house, facing east. Content now, Peter began stroking the animal's head and shoulders, thrilling to the dog's eager response to his every touch. It was as though the dog could not get enough fast enough. The boy petted faster, using both hands, as though he could not give enough, fast enough.

The bond between boy and animal begun the day before was sealed in the heavy darkness of that particular morning. They became a match, a pair, together something they could never be apart. The raw emotion poured endlessly from the boy. The dog absorbed it all and wanted more. Peter was happy as the warm, wet tongue of the dog caressed his burning cheek.

Peter would have been content to remain there forever. The long moment of silent communion passed before he noticed that it was no longer dark around him. Glancing up in surprise, his eyes were drawn to a sight he had never seen before. Colors, beautiful iridescent colors streaking and blending together across the eastern sky. His face aglow with wonder at the sight of the unfolding sunrise, Peter watched, transfixed, as the deep, rich reds and blues turned to lighter hues of pinks, yellows, and blue greys. It was a symphony of light and color spreading in living panorama before him. A cosmic announcement that something spectacular was about to occur. With the dog hugged firmly against his chest, the boy felt a strange, new excitement begin to swell within him as the heavenly display continued, drawing him ever nearer the dawning event. At the moment of his greatest expectation the colors began melting away from the horizon, leaving in their place a brighter light. For a moment time stood still. And then it came. The first bit of bright red sun appeared suddenly above the horizon through the trees on the mountaintop only a short distance away. It was the beginning climax of a magnificent cosmic drama. Peter exploded into a joyful cheer, clapping his hands and laughing excitedly as he rocked back and forth with the dog. His eyes were radiant with joy.

Peter had never seen anything like that sunrise, nor had he ever felt so excited about an event that involved no adults. It made him feel good. And warm. And secure. It was so natural and beautiful. Though this was his first experienced sunrise, he somehow knew it was the same every morning. Every day began with it. Not a day would pass without it. It was permanent. He could count on it. No matter what else might happen, he could count on the sun rising each morning. It was the first certainty he ever consciously knew.

The thrill of that morning never left Peter. It only became subdued in the harsh light of unending days filled with real people, real problems, and real fears. But it was renewed each morning as life itself was renewed by the warmth of a majestic, benevolent sun.

It was then Peter named the dog "Bo." Short for "beautiful." The sunrise and the dog. Both were beautiful. It fit.

"Peter? Pe—e—eter!" the voice called out the kitchen window. "Come on in for breakfast!"

It was Mrs. Jones. Peter had been so engrossed in the sunrise that he had forgotten all about the others and he had not heard the rattle of coffeepot and skillet on the stove.

Like an egg cracked hard above a frying pan, the boy felt the happiness pour out of him and become something else. His time with Bo was over. Although he knew it was best to obey, he left with a deep yearning to return and a belief that Bo would be waiting for him.

"You stay here and be a good boy," he spoke kindly to the animal. "I'll be back in a little while."

Getting to his feet reluctantly, Peter moved to the back porch of the house with Bo at his heels. Bobby met him at the door with an anxious question.

"Where have you been, Peter? I looked everywhere for you and I couldn't find you. I didn't know where you were." Then he saw the dog still on the back porch, and his eyes lit up as memories of yesterday returned. Reaching around Peter, he tried to pet the dog.

"He's my dog, Bobby!" exclaimed Peter, stepping again between the dog and his brother. "Bo is my dog. You leave him alone."

There was something in his brother's voice that made the younger boy step back into the kitchen. Peter followed as Bo stretched himself out by the door, his head just high enough from that position to allow him to see into the room through the screen mesh.

Jimmy was there in the kitchen too. Not knowing what else to do, the three uneasy boys stood awkwardly along the wall and watched the busy farm woman prepare breakfast. Slicing long strips of bacon from the salted slab hanging from a hook in the pantry beside the stove, she soon had bacon and eggs frying, coffee perking, and biscuits baking in the oven.

"Mornin', boys," she greeted them.

"Good mornin'," they answered reluctantly in turn.

"You boys sleep all right?"

"Yes, ma'am," Jimmy answered for them.

"Well, that's fine," she exclaimed. "Bet you boys are hungry, aren't you?"

No one answered this time. Peter did not answer for fear of revealing his vulnerability.

Appearing not to notice, she began filling two plates beside the stove with crisp, sizzling bacon, eggs fried sunny side up, and hot, buttered biscuits. Peter watched her eagerly, his stomach growling uncontrollably. It all looked and smelled good. Anxiously he awaited the invitation to sit down and eat.

About ready to eat, the woman told the boys to wash up.

Following her instructions carefully, Peter dipped two—no more—ladles of water from the water bucket beside the sink into a small wash basin.

Even now, in 1957, the farm was without running water and relied on monthly deliveries of butane for cooking fuel. The house was heated by a wood-burning stove. Toilet facilities were in an outhouse a hundred yards to the south of the house. Drinking and cooking water had to be carried in gallon jars and buckets to the house from an artesian well on the bank of the river, a distance of about a mile. This was a daily task no one relished. Water was not to be wasted.

Taking turns, the boys washed their hands under the watchful eye of the woman, drying them vigorously on a small towel she provided. Once finished, Peter was instructed to toss the water out the back door.

At the stroke of seven Mr. Jones came into the kitchen through the back door. Replacing his straw hat on the nail beside the door, he moved quickly to the sink to accomplish for himself the task just completed by the boys.

"Mornin', boys," he greeted them as they stood against the far wall of the kitchen watching him.

"Good morning," they answered his greeting.

"You boys can eat in here," the woman said as she set three small plates on the kitchen table pushed into one corner of the room. They watched eagerly as she placed two small biscuits on each of the three plates. These were followed by a small pat of butter and two tablespoons of light corn syrup. Taking a knife, she blended the butter and syrup until they were a smooth, creamy mixture.

"OK, boys, sit down and have at it."

Eagerly the boys raced to claim a chair at the table. Once seated they waited, not knowing what to do next. There was no silverware beside the plates except a knife. Confused, Peter watched as she carried two full plates of biscuits, eggs and bacon into the dining room. She returned for steaming cups of coffee, a large bowl of jelly, and a jar of honey. Then they were gone, and the boys were alone with their meager meal in the kitchen. The boys heard their guardians begin eating heartily in the other room.

Still unsure of themselves, the boys looked first at the two small biscuits on their plates and then at each other. As before, Peter could read the question in his younger brothers' eyes. After a moment he shrugged his shoulders and picked up a biscuit from the plate. Awkwardly using the knife, he spread some of the butter-syrup mixture on the biscuit and took a bite. It tasted good. Real good. Following the example of their older brother, the younger boys were soon wolfing down their biscuits. In a moment there was not a scrap or crumb of biscuit left on any of the three plates.

Afraid to move, and not knowing what to do next, the boys sat around the empty table, waiting, and silently watching each other while listening attentively to the idle conversation that came and went in spurts from the other room. The smell of eggs and bacon still clung to the kitchen, making them feel hungrier now than before they had eaten the biscuits.

After what seemed to the boys like an eternity of waiting, the couple in the other room finished their meal. Mrs. Jones reappeared in the kitchen with an armload of dirty dishes.

"OK, boys. Peter, I want you to wash up these dishes. You younger boys go play," she directed as she set the dishes on the drainboard.

Slowly and unenthusiastically the two smaller boys climbed down off their chairs and moved hesitantly toward the screen door. Before stepping out into the backyard they glanced curiously over their shoulders to see if there was any food left among the second load of dishes carried from the dining room to the kitchen. There wasn't.

Mr. Jones entered the kitchen and moved directly to the water bucket sitting on the drainboard to the left of the chipped porcelain sink with no faucets and removed the large drinking dipper from its nail on the wall. Probing deep into the cool, dark liquid, he raised the full, dripping dipper to his thirsty lips. As he drank, his eyes sought the world outside the window above the sink. Though a practical man with little time for idle pleasures, he paid a long, silent tribute to whatever power made mornings like this one possible and then allowed his mind to return to the more practical concerns of farm life. Like a king surveying his kingdom, his eyes roamed the length and breadth of the barnyard before him, and beyond. He owned everything in sight. All was quiet and as it should be. Satisfied, he moved from the window and out of the way of the small boy slinking nervously around him.

"I'm goin' to the barn," he called out to no one in particular, grabbing his hat off its nail along the way.

Having gotten the dishwater ready in the same small basin used earlier to wash hands, Mrs. Jones ushered Peter to the sink. There he was instructed to wash all the silverware and utensils first, then the dishes, and finally the pots, pans, and skillets. After the washing procedure was finished, he was to toss the soapy water into the backyard and refill the basin with clean water in which to rinse the dishes. They were then to be placed into the drain on the right of the sink and left there to dry.

"Be sure to get them clean now," she commanded. "If there is one thing I cannot stand it is sloppiness—particularly with dishes we have to eat off of. And make sure you do everything just as I told you."

Stepping back to watch the boy labor at his unfamiliar task, she seemed satisfied and moved toward another part of the house.

"After you finish the dishes, Peter, there are a few chores I want you to do," she said in the wake of her departure from the room.

Peter sighed in relief when the woman was gone. Having finished washing the silverware, cups, and glasses, he now moved to the short stack of dirty plates. Reaching for the top one he noticed some yolk from the fried eggs still clinging to the plate, interspersed with tiny bread crumbs. On one side of the plate was a blue smear left by a blob of jelly.

For a moment the plate in his hand hovered uncertainly above the surface of the soapy dish water. Then in a moment of decision, Peter licked the plate clean.

[Chapter Seven]

The dog days of August, 1957, melted one into another with little notice of their differences. The excessive heat and problems of harvesting were the major topics of conversation.

Peter did not take long to adapt to farm life. In reality, he had little choice. Unlike the other foster homes where few responsibilities were placed upon him, there was a great deal of work to be done on the farm and he was expected to do his share. His list of chores grew almost daily for the first few weeks until they amounted to a daily routine demanding much of his attention and most of his time.

Emotionally Peter was a mixture of rage and resignation. Blaming himself bitterly for allowing the deputy sheriff and welfare worker to take him away from his mother, he accepted his fate helplessly. Running away was out of the question because he was several hours by car from his mother. He could never make it on foot. It was his own fault. He deserved nothing less than what he got. On the other hand, he was angry. Angry at adults, particularly those who held any authority over him. Though never openly hostile or disobedient, his anger took shape as resentment, resistance to adult wishes, and an occasional rebellious outburst, though covert, of domestic sabotage. He did not like adults. Nor did he trust them. He wanted to stay as far away from them as possible, interacting and communicating with them only when necessary to fulfill his needs. His attention and affections were turned away from adults towards his brothers, Bo, and the magic world of nature.

Within days of their arrival on the farm, Peter and his brothers were well drilled in the rules they were expected to obey. They were foster kids—children no one else wanted—who were living on the farm as guests. If they did not behave, they were told, they would be sent to live with the niggers in the woods across the river who ate white children.

Mrs. Jones was the disciplinarian and watched over their conduct like a hawk stalking prey. Their every move was measured, every action weighed in terms of financial gain or loss to the family.

Each boy was provided a wardrobe consisting of two short sleeved shirts, two long sleeved woolen shirts, two pair of blue jeans, one jean jacket, one pair of boots, three pair of underwear, three pair of socks, one belt, and one pair of cutoffs. During the long days of summer they were allowed to wear nothing but the cutoffs, not even underwear. Only at school and on occasional trips into the community were they allowed to wear underwear, and a shirt with their cutoffs in summer and their jeans in winter. Shoes and socks were worn only on special occasions and during particularly cold weather. At all other times they went barefoot.

The farmhouse in which they lived was small, consisting of three bedrooms, a living room, dining room, and kitchen. There were several walk-in closets used for storage. All three boys slept in the same bed in one of the bedrooms. The other two bedrooms, one of which was reserved for the occasional visits of the Joneses' three grown children, were off limits to the boys except when sent there to do a chore. The boys were allowed only to sleep and eat in the house during the warm days, and only on the coldest days of winter. During the summer their playground became the hundreds of acres of farmland, pastures, and forests that made up the farm. They all but lived in the barn amidst its towering stacks of baled hay during the winter.

The boys were bathed twice a year, once in the spring and once in the fall. The only other contact with soap and water took place during the many occasions of wading and splashing in the river and ponds.

They were not allowed to use the outhouse. All biological functions were expected to be performed somewhere far away from the house, preferably in the forest. Only two squares—no more—of toilet paper were allowed per occasion. Violation of this rule would result in no toilet paper being allowed for one week. Leaves became a common and necessary substitute.

Clothes washing occurred once a month during the summer, seldom during the colder times of year. It was a job that took most of the day. After he had observed Mrs. Jones a couple of times, Peter performed the task alone. Wash day always began by carrying pails full of pond water to fill the big black kettle in the backyard, which took many trips because the pail was small and the kettle large. Then he would gather wood and build a roaring fire under the kettle so that the water would be hot by the time he had finished his breakfast chores. After gathering the clothes, he would dump them into the boiling water along with a bar of homemade lye soap, stirring them occasionally with a large poking stick. While the clothes were boiling, he would carry more pails of pond water to fill the large aluminum washtub sitting on the back porch. Removing the clothes piece by piece from the boiling pot using the poking stick, he would rinse them in the clean water and lay them to dry across the top of the fence separating the house from the barnyard. The articles of clothing would be left there all day and then collected and folded in the late afternoon. Wash day was always a busy day for Peter.

Under the watchful eyes of Mrs. Jones, the house with its many domestic necessities became the primary arena of Peter's labor. Beginning with the first day, the cleanup chores after meals became his responsibility. Others were soon added. Within days of his arrival he became responsible for setting the table for meals, making all the beds, and keeping the linoleumed floors swept, mopped, and waxed.

Peter hated these chores. He hated Mrs. Jones's constant surveillance. He hated being inside when what he wanted most was to be outside in the bright light of a fading summer, free to chase his fantasies through the endless adventures he imagined were a natural part of the world he could see awaiting him just beyond the corral fences. He wanted to be outside, alone, away from her. But mostly, he wanted to be with Bo.

The chore he resented most was the one which earned him a nickname he despised. Every morning he was expected to empty the chamber pot kept overnight in the Joneses' bedroom. Since there was no running water in the house, there were no toilet facilities indoors. The chamber pot was a necessary convenience for Mrs. Jones.

One morning as Peter, swelling with rage and resentment, was carrying the chamber pot at arm's length in front of him through the house on his way to the back door, he accidentally (on purpose) spilled its contents all over the hardwood living room floor. Mrs. Jones heard the metal clang of the pot hitting the floor and knew instantly what had happened. Her eyes blazing with anger, she burst in on the boy standing belligerent and frightened in the middle of the mess. She carried a belt in her hand. Grabbing him by the arm, she let the full weight of her displeasure be felt as the belt lashed angrily at the back of his bare legs.

Stung by the pain, Peter tried to jerk free of her hold and dart past the angry woman. Instead, she forced him to his knees in the middle of the mess and threw old towels down in front of him.

"Clean it up, you little piss ant!" she screamed at him.

From that day onward Peter had a nickname. Though she would never use it except when angry, she was angry at him enough for the nickname to become an indelible part of his young identity; a descriptive term that both named and described him.

Unbeknownst to Mrs. Jones at first, another tradition was begun that day. From that day onward until he was caught, Peter made a point of emptying the chamber pot off the side of the front porch instead of in the field behind the barn as he was instructed to do. It was not until the middle of the following summer, when the heat was at its worst, that she finally figured out what was causing that awful stench around the front porch—and why the grass on that side of the porch would not grow.

As the oldest of the three boys, Peter was responsible for the care of his brothers: to put them to bed at eight o'clock sharp, to get them up in the mornings, and to make sure they were dressed, fed, and fell into no harm. This chore he accepted gladly. Parenting his brothers was the only chore that came naturally, and the only one he did not resent. It helped him act out his own need for care and attention. He applied himself to the task eagerly. Due to the strictness of Mrs. Jones and her many rules, Peter soon engineered new and clandestine methods for achieving fulfillment, to his discriminating satisfaction, of this particular responsibility. He learned to pilfer food from the pantry for them to eat, to steal pennies and chewing gum from the sewing box he had discovered buried in Mrs. Jones's closet, and to lie in order to protect his brothers from her bristling and retaliatory anger. He became quite good at all three.

Eventually Peter was assigned more chores. By early September he had been taught how to cook breakfast, which soon became a permanent job. The boys were fed only twice a day when not in school. Breakfast during the entire three years they remained on the farm was the same every day except for those rare occasions when there was company in the house. On those days Mrs. Jones would prepare the meal, alter the menu accordingly, and allow the boys to share in the feast, though they still had to eat in the kitchen away from the adults. She would even wash the dishes. What holidays these were for Peter! On every other day, however, he was expected to climb up on the small wooden stool placed in front of the stove for his use and cook a breakfast of bacon, eggs, and biscuits for his guardians. He and his brothers were never allowed more than the usual two biscuits. And, of course, he always had to wash the dishes after the meal.

There was never a lunch. Dinner was generally hearty, however, usually consisting of canned or fresh vegetables, depending on the season of the year, cornbread, beans, and fried potatoes and gravy. Meat was served only on Sundays when a chicken would be killed and fried. Combined with mashed potatoes, gravy, green beans, fresh tomatoes, biscuits, and cake for dessert, it was an event the boys looked forward to every week.

Always hungry, it seemed, the boys learned early how to steal watermelons, cantaloupes, tomatoes, and cucumbers from the garden during its season. They learned to recognize edible berries and the several kinds of fruit on the trees about the farm. During the winter they would eat cattle cake, grain, and the dried chunks of bread and salted pork scraps stored in the smokehouse for the dogs. Egg shells, coffee grounds, butter wrappers, and scraps of discarded food were pillaged from the garbage as a regular addition to their diet.

Peter learned how to sneak pieces of cake, and bread, dried fruit, and other scraps of food out of the kitchen to his brothers. Occasionally he was able to manage a small amount of sugar, jelly, honey, or sorghum. These were what his brothers liked most.

Peter's first attempt at making gravy unsupervised was a disaster. He was not sure how much flour was needed to thicken the gravy to a palatable consistency. With two tablespoons of bacon grease remaining in the skillet, he mixed in four tablespoons of flour. After then adding the milk, the result was a gravy too thick to eat.

Dismayed, Peter did not know what to do with his mistake. He knew that he was forbidden to throw away food.

Desperately he sought a way to be rid of the unwanted paste in the skillet before Mrs. Jones found out about it. He was afraid to throw it in the garbage for fear she would find it. About that time his brothers came in and Peter had his solution. Or so he thought. Sitting his brothers down at the kitchen table, he dipped each a healthy portion of the gravy and urged them to eat it. As hungry as they were, both refused vehemently with only an exploratory taste, escaping headlong out the back door before he could stop them. Insulted and frustrated, he turned to the only other source of help he could think of at the time—the dogs. Like the boys, the farm dogs were maintained on a meager diet and were always anxious for something to eat. They would eat anything. Well, almost anything. Emptying the contents of the skillet into a large feeding dish, he was mobbed by hungry dogs as they saw him appear on the back porch with that dish which meant food in his hands. Peter was shocked as he watched one dog after another take his turn at the dish, only to sniff once and then move slowly away with tail and head drooping in obvious disappointment. Not even the starving dogs would eat his gravy! Peter finally emptied the gravy under the house and covered it with loose dirt, hoping desperately that Mrs. Jones would have no reason to be under the house any time soon.

As time went on Peter was also expected to assist with some of the farm chores, such as gathering the eggs and milking. As he grew older he would ride the baler during haying season, assist with the branding, drive a tractor during the plowing season, and heave bales of hay out of the moving pickup during the daily winter feeding of livestock.

During those first few weeks on the farm, however, the only chore that took him out of the house and away from Mrs. Jones was hauling the water. One day she placed six empty gallon jars in a small, rusty wagon she kept stored in the smokehouse for her grandchildren to play with on their occasional visits. With Peter pulling the wagon and Bo at his heels, she led him the distance from the house to the artesian well near the river. There she showed him how to stand on the rock near the single pipe protruding at an angle from the ground and fill the jars one by one with fresh water pouring endlessly from the pipe. Then, with wagon loaded down, she once again led the way as Peter pulled the now heavy wagon back to the house. Satisfied that he could manage the chore alone, Mrs. Jones unceremoniously awarded him the task, cautioning him pointedly that it must be done every morning without fail, before breakfast if possible.

It was the hardest job Peter had to do. His eight-year-old muscles would strain hard against the heavy load. The trip to the river with the empty jars was a joy ride compared to the agonizing trip back. But he did not mind this chore as much as the others, for two reasons: he was outside and away from Mrs. Jones, and he was with Bo.

Bo was his constant companion. There was not a place that Peter went that the faithful, loving dog did not accompany him. They were inseparable. Peter's love for the animal grew daily until he loved it more than any other living thing, apart from his brothers.

After the morning chores were completed, he and Bo would often roam the forest along the river, playing tag with each other and chasing around boulders and trees, always ending up beside each other on a clump of grass in the shade of a towering tree. There they would sit enjoying each other's company.

They even found a special tree they called their own. It was tall with branches spread wide across the river. Peter would often climb to the very top of it and sit in a perch formed by connecting branches. He could see for miles from there. The farm, the pastures, the endless river winding its way lazily through the forest, the road leading to and from the farm. It soon became his favorite place in all the world. A place that only he and Bo knew about and shared together. He loved it.

Sometimes he felt better sitting in that tree. It was as

though he could see everything around him from up there, everything that moved, everything that was happening, or might happen. Nothing could surprise him with such a view from such a position, or catch him off guard.

In fulfilling the task of hauling water before breakfast, Peter and Bo would drag the wagonload of empty jars to the river while it was still dark. Parking the wagon at the base of their tree, Peter would leave Bo settled snugly upon a clump of grass nearby and climb to his perch high in the branches. There he would wait, and watch, as once again the morning sun would push itself reassuringly above the distant horizon.

It became his special moment—a time when he and Bo could be alone, together, at their special place, to experience the essence of life and each other in the presence of a love so extraordinary that its image would appear each morning painted across the eastern sky. Those times became his treasure.

The soft murmur of the river in the background now supplied music for the symphony of color that welcomed him each morning. The tears that often flowed painfully down his cheeks could not wash away the smile that returned the morning's greeting as the bright red and orange tip of sun first appeared. Occasionally, like the first time, he would laugh and cheer with its coming, that strange, new excitement swelling uncontrollably within him once more. At other times he would just sit quietly, watching and listening and feeling.

All too soon he would have to climb down from the tree, collect the wagon and Bo, and continue on his way. There were chores to be done.

[Chapter Eight]

Almost without knowing it, Peter found himself in school. In September of his first year on the farm, he began third grade.

The school was located five miles west of the farm in a small rural village. It was a small country school serving the many farm families in the area. Three buildings made up the educational complex: one building contained the cafeteria, and the other two buildings each had three classrooms. Each classroom housed two grades and one teacher. One building was for grades one through six, the other for grades seven through twelve.

The principal's wife, Mrs. Adams, taught third and fourth grades. She was an unusually attractive woman with a warm smile and gentle touch. Something about her reminded Peter of his mother. Her eyes maybe. Or her soft, melodious voice. Whatever it was drew him irresistibly to her. He wanted to be near her. He wanted her to touch him—or at least notice him with a smile.

Within weeks of the start of classes, Peter worked his way into a special position in the class. He was her pet. He worked so hard to fulfill her every request that she could not help paying special attention to him. Though he was quiet and withdrawn among the other students, seldom participating in their activities on the playground or in the classroom, Peter completed his academic work in an effortless outpouring of natural ability. Within a few weeks, she discovered that he could complete by noon the list of assignments written on the chalkboard each morning as that day's work. Unless she made a special effort to provide him more work, he spent the afternoons looking at books or drawing pictures. Deciding to channel his extra energy and time into more constructive pursuits, Mrs. Adams made him a teacher's helper and put him to work in the afternoons tutoring other students in reading and arithmetic, grading papers, running errands for her, or working in the yard and garden surrounding her house across the street. At the age of eight, Peter had begun working for wages.

Because of the extra attention and responsibility given him by the teacher, he became something of a celebrity at school. The other children seemed to respect him, envy him, and avoid him. For a while that suited him fine. He wanted to be left alone anyway. By being moved from one foster home to another so many times, he had already attended so many schools with so many children that he had no desire to get to know these. All he wanted was to be alone.

Peter liked school. It got him away from the farm, his chores, and Mrs. Jones. His only regret was that Bo could not come to school with him.

Mrs. Adams had seemed different from Mrs. Jones from the first day. He felt good and somehow special when she praised his work in front of the class. Within days, he had a crush on her and was eager to do anything to please her. He had thrilled inwardly when she had invited him to become her helper. It was a deal, just between the two of them. The specialness of that bond more than made up for the many long hours he spent alone, hot, and sweating in her garden across the street. He wanted badly for her to like him as much as he liked her.

Occasionally at the end of a week, she would place a quarter in the palm of his hand as payment for his labors. It was hard, at those times, for him to believe he was worth that much. Several times he wondered if she really knew the value of what she was giving him. So much, and all at once! He adored her.

Proud of his earnings, Peter would carry the quarter tightly in the palm of his hand throughout the long bus ride back to the farm. The route through the countryside always began and ended at the farm. He was the first to be picked up in the mornings and the last returned home in the evenings. He would show the money to Mrs. Jones, who would take the quarter, place it in a white envelope, and stick the envelope in the cavity of her pedal sewing machine for safekeeping. This she did with every penny Peter earned, and he never saw any of it again. Since he was forbidden to touch the sewing machine, he never checked to see if it was still there, and he never thought to ask for it back.

Fall that year slowly surrended its hold on the country as

the freezing grip of winter forced its way across the land. The countryside lay buried in snow for weeks. The gravel roads were slick and hazardous, but school was not interrupted. The only difference was that the children were allowed outside the school buildings for very brief periods during the day. On the coldest days, recess was canceled altogether. On those days, the teacher would substitute a classroom activity in the place of recess. Spelling bees, games, speed math contests, and skits were common, and the students enjoyed them.

One day late in January, the teacher announced a new contest for the class to replace their afternoon recess.

"Class," she called, "we have been talking for several weeks now about how important it is for boys and girls to be well groomed and use good hygiene. So, let's find out if we have any well-groomed boys and girls in our class this afternoon."

The children giggled, shifting nervously in their seats as they waited for the contest to begin. As was usually the case, the girls were first. The teacher called them to the front of the room and had them stand in a straight line in front of the chalkboard, facing the boys.

"All right, boys," Mrs. Adams began, "we are now going to vote on who we think is the prettiest and most well-groomed girl in our class. Any questions?"

There were none.

The girls stood silently with every eye glued to some special spot on the floor as the boys studied them with new and critical eyes.

The first vote was unanimous. The prettiest and most well-groomed girl in the class was decided to be Rebecca. Soft brown hair falling loosely across her shoulders and back, smiling brown eyes, deep dimples, and a bright red sash tied snugly around her waist made her an easy winner. Besides, she was a lousy marble player and would always let one of the boys pinch kick for her in the kickball games at recess. That was all it took as far as the boys were concerned.

The voting continued for second, third, fourth places,

and on until there were only three girls left standing dejectedly before the class. Out of consideration for their feelings, the teacher dismissed them, without a vote, to return to their seats.

After the last girl was again seated and sought anonymity within the sea of faces, the teacher again faced the class.

"Now, girls. It is your turn to vote for the most handsome and well-groomed boy in the class. Boys, to the front."

As the girls had done before them, the boys shuffled slowly to the front of the room, lining up awkwardly along the length of the blackboard.

Although Peter could not bring himself to look out at the girls, he was sure they were all watching him. There was no doubt in his mind that he would be chosen the most handsome and well-groomed boy in the class. After all, he was the teacher's helper. In his mind, that was all it took. Still, he could not help fidgeting, first on one foot and then on the other, back and forth, with his hands plunged as far as they would go into his pockets. He counted the number of colored dots on the square of tile in front of his feet three times before the voting finally started.

Like the boys, the girls were unanimous in their choice. The teacher made the announcement.

"The girls have chosen David as the most handsome and well-groomed boy in our class," she proclaimed.

All eyes followed the surprised boy as he moved quickly to reclaim his seat. Peter was stunned. What had happened? He had never thought about being handsome and well groomed before. Nor had he cared what the other children thought about him before. But he cared then. He cared a great deal. Suddenly he needed their approval badly.

After a moment, the voting continued. Second place went to Joe, third to Mike, fourth to Ronnie, fifth to Bobby, sixth to . . . , and on it went until there were only three boys left standing at the front of the class. The teacher dismissed the three, without a vote, ordering them back to their seats. Peter was one of them.

By the time he had reclaimed his seat among the other students, Peter was sure that every person in the class thought he was ugly, even Mrs. Adams. What must she think of him now? He had wanted so desperately for her to like him. Now, he knew that was impossible.

[Chaper Nine]

By spring of that first year, life on the farm had become routine for Peter. Each day was basically the same. Up before dawn, he would make his daily trip with Bo to the artesian well for water, return to the farm in time to prepare his brothers for school, and cook breakfast for the family. He was instructed to awaken the Joneses with a hot cup of coffee before serving breakfast, no later than seven o'clock. By seven-thirty, the meal would be completed. Peter had just enough time then before the school bus arrived to wash the dishes and empty the chamber pot. If he hurried through the chores, he would have a few minutes to spend alone with Bo before leaving for school. He did his other chores after school and on weekends.

When Peter was not outside, Bo spent most of his time during the cold days of winter curled in a warm, furry ball in a corner under the back porch. Crawling on his stomach, Peter had just enough room to fit under the small porch too. He had carried several empty feed sacks from the barn to place under the porch in order to make a warm bed for Bo. Some he used to cover himself against the penetrating cold when he was there with Bo. Many long, winter weekend hours were spent huddled together under that back porch. He would often fall asleep with his head resting securely on the dog's shank. Peter felt safe in their private little hiding place under the back porch. His brothers were afraid to crawl through the small opening for fear of the darkness there. Mrs. Jones would never think to look for him there. It was the perfect place for them.

Because of the snow and cold, he and Bo had all but ceased their endless wanderings about the countryside. The need to stay warm drove them to seek shelter from the elements. Peter yearned for the return of warm weather so that they could resume their morning vigil at the tree and once again know the freedom of a world that welcomed them as its own. He felt more comfortable alone with Bo in the woods than he did in the company of the Joneses in the house. He knew from experience that his relationship with them was only temporary, that sooner or later he and his brothers would be removed to another home. It had always happened that way, and he was sure it would happen that way again. Like a man on death row awaiting the inevitable, Peter lived out his sentence on the farm one day at a time, obediently fulfilling his responsibilities while avoiding all unnecessary contact with his guardians. His pleasures he sought in the world around him, with his brothers and Bo. He felt like a stranger on the farm, like a hired hand that could stay only so long as he was needed to do chores. He did not feel as though he really belonged there.

Until one Saturday, early in May. The day dawned bright and clear. The winter snows were long gone, and the farm was busy with spring activities. The world around him was flush with new life in an atmosphere of warm expectancy.

After Peter washed the breakfast dishes and left them on the drainboard to dry, Mrs. Jones called the three boys together in the kitchen. They stood self-consciously against the wall, watching her cautiously, afraid they were in trouble again.

Sitting down at the table with a cup of coffee in front of her, Mrs. Jones eyed the boys critically. Then she spoke.

"Now, boys, in a little while a bus load of kids from a school in the city will be coming to visit us. Karen—you've heard me talk about Karen, she's my oldest daughter—is their teacher. Anyway, since these kids live in the city, most of them have never visited a farm before. They have never been around farm animals before. So, Karen is bringing them on a field trip."

Suddenly, Peter was all ears. There were other kids coming to the farm—his farm. Somehow, the news bothered him. He did not like the thought of their invading his world. What if they found his hideout under the back porch? Or his tree near the river? What if they liked Bo and wanted to take him home with them? The thought of having to compete with other children on the farm frightened him. Suddenly he wanted to take Bo and run away.

"Now," Mrs. Jones continued, that look of stern command showing on her face, "they are bringing picnic lunches with them. At lunchtime they are all going to sit down in the front yard to eat their sack lunches. I want you boys to get all the dogs and lock them up under the house until the kids have finished eating. All of them. You know how those mangy dogs are. They'll eat anything in sight. We can't have that. So you boys lock them under the house and keep them there. Do you understand me?"

Peter was hurt to think he would have to lock Bo under the house. Bo would not hurt any of those kids, and he could make sure that the animal did not bother them at lunch. It was not fair. Already his mind was at work thinking where he could hide Bo so that he would not have to be locked under the house with the other dogs.

"Yes, ma'am," the boys answered in unison.

"All right then. I want you boys to help me keep an eye on those kids to make sure none of them wander off and get lost or hurt. And don't you dare let me catch any of you being mean to them," she concluded with a long look that meant business. "All right, go get those dogs locked up."

The boys scurried to do as commanded. It took the better part of an hour, but at last the resistant dogs were under the house. Bo was the last to be pushed through the small opening in the foundation of the house. Peter replaced the grill regretfully, apologizing to the dog sorrowfully as he did so.

Peter and his brothers watched from the porch as the bus load of kids unloaded near the front gate a short time later. Slowly the city kids congregated in a group near the door of the bus, scanning the scene around them as though bewildered by what they saw. Mr. and Mrs. Jones were in the midst of them, laughing and talking their welcome excitedly.

Peter curiously watched the boys and girls. Though they were about his own age, they seemed shy and unsure of themselves, waiting to be told what to do. All of them wore pants, a shirt, and shoes. Their hair was combed and their clothes clean. Peter became aware of how different he and his brothers would look among them wearing only their cutoffs. He felt self-conscious.

After introductions and a welcome, Mrs. Jones assigned Peter the task of showing a group of the kids around the farm. She gave strict orders that he was to keep them away from the river and corralled animals.

Obediently but disdainfully, Peter moved off with a group of boys and girls. Before leaving the yard, he let Bo out from under the house, careful not to allow the others out at the same time. Bo trotted merrily in front of them, leading the way.

"That your dog?" asked one little girl, pointing to Bo.

"Bo ain't nobody's dog," Peter answered defensively, stopping long enough to hug the dog's neck. "He's my friend. Me and Bo don't belong to nobody."

Peter soon discovered how gullible the city kids were. They would believe anything he told them. He had their undivided attention. Warming to his task as tour guide, he let his eight-year-old imagination come alive and take charge. He shared many fantasies secretively with them as they moved from one farm attraction to another. He was encouraged to continue when they gasped nervously with fear and admiration as he told them just how exciting and dangerous living on a farm really was—assuring them on the way that they were safe with him. He told them of floods and killer tornados, of giant chicken snakes waiting in the tall grass around the chicken house for their chance to snatch away an unsuspecting hen and carry her to their den in the woods where they would swallow her alive, of wild bobcats and bears roaming freely in the forests, of wolves coming to the back door of the house at supper time. He told them about the gold hidden by outlaws somewhere in the rocks near his tree. And how someday he and Bo were going to find the treasure and become rich. In a great act of sharing, he even told them about the secret wishing well of the Indians he had discovered one day by accident in the forest. All you had to do was drop a penny into the well while chanting the mysterious incantation that only he knew, and your wish would come true magically.

The girls particularly were intrigued by this and crowded around him, eagerly asking to be taken there so they could make their own wishes. Their youthfully feminine eyes filled with yearning and deep admiration as he calmly explained the dangers of such a trip and suggested valiantly that he would risk the journey himself—alone—on their behalf. His heroic gallantry made them gasp their adoration.

By the time Peter had returned the kids to the barnyard where they could pet animals and ride horses, he was a hero. A hero that had collected six pennies and twice as many wishes for his trouble.

But the living fairy tale came to an abrupt end when one of the little girls, his most vocal admirer, raced excitedly to her teacher to share the good news. As her face clouded, Karen sought out her mother and reported what Peter had done.

Mrs. Jones's anger was fueled into fury at the sight of Bo running loose among the children. Taking Peter by the ear, Mrs. Jones make him return the pennies to their owners and apologize for lying. Then she banished him under the house with the dogs until the picnic was over and the kids were on their way back to the city. She ushered the dog under the house right behind him.

Peter and the dogs crowded around the foundation grill looking into the front yard where the children were settling themselves on the grass to eat lunch. Chattering excitedly about their many adventures, they began spreading their lunches, item by item, around them.

Though still smarting from his recent run-in with Mrs. Jones, Peter envied the children in the front yard. He was jealous. They were doing things on the farm he had never been allowed to do, such as riding the horses and having a picnic lunch. He never had lunch. Let alone a picnic. It was not fair. He was angry and resented the children even being there. If it were not for them, he and Bo would not have been locked under the house with the dogs. He wanted them to go away and leave him alone.

While he watched, the little girl who had told on him bit into a fried chicken leg. Looking up as she chewed, she caught sight of Peter behind the iron grill inches off the ground. Smiling, she waved at him. Resentfully, Peter did not wave back. Suddenly the smile vanished and she stuck her tongue out at him. That did it! Without a moment's thought for consequences, Peter called the horde of dogs with him to the opening at the back of the house. Removing the grill carefully, he was mobbed as the dogs fought to get out.

A dozen dogs, barking wildly, poured into the peaceful setting in the front yard. Racing from one cluster of children to another, they grabbed at every piece of food they could find. The kids scrambled to their feet, screaming in terror and running from the hungry dogs. Some were sent sprawling on the grass as they tried to get to their feet. It was a madhouse. Food, kids, adults, and dogs were flying everywhere. Peter was particularly gratified to see the chicken leg still clutched in the little girl's hand disappear in a blur of streaking animal fur.

After the food was gone, the dogs were chased away and the children were herded hurriedly, one by one, onto the bus. In an attempt to make amends, Mrs. Jones climbed aboard the bus as its engine roared to life and gave each of the wide-eyed kids a horse shoe as a souvenir of their visit to the farm. In moments they were on their way back to the city.

After they were gone, Mr. Jones headed resolutely to the barn without a word. Mrs. Jones headed straight for Peter. Seeing her coming, Peter tried to scurry under the back porch before she saw him, hoping to be safe in his hiding place.

A split second more and he would have made it; she would have had to tear the back porch apart to get at him. But as it was, she was able to grab hold of his foot just before it disappeared and drag him out from under the porch amidst a barrage of curses.

Peter was thrashed soundly with the end of a lariat and put to work cleaning up every scrap of paper and trash left in the front yard. Her angry words echoed in his ears all afternoon.

His cleanup chore finally completed, Peter disappeared with Bo for the rest of the afternoon. Unbeknownst to Mrs. Jones, they were sitting inside a corral feeding green persimmons to Blackie, the milk cow. Though he had been told never to feed her green persimmons because they would dry up her milk, Peter did not care. Not then anyway. She wanted the green persimmons, so he let her have them.

Several days later when Mrs. Jones went to do the milking she discovered the cow dry. She wondered about it for only a moment before she knew why. And she knew who.

[Chapter Ten]

Halloween, Thanksgiving, Christmas, and New Year's Day all came and went unnoticed by Peter that first year. None of the Joneses' three children and several grandchildren came home for the holidays. As a result, there were no special meals, presents, or celebrations. The only exposure to the festivities of these occasions Peter gained was at school. Mrs. Adams would have the class draw and color pictures depicting the season and hang them on the walls of the classroom as decorations. Occasionally, she would read a story of ghosts and goblins, pilgrims, or Santa Claus to the class. Peter would listen curiously to the other children chatter excitedly about their holiday experiences once school reconvened. For Peter the holidays meant nothing more than a painful memory of a time long ago and a few days out of school. By the time he was old enough to really care about such things and take an interest in them, his father and mother had already separated and his mother was living on welfare. There was never enough money then for such extravagant things as Christmas presents, trees, or holiday decorations. Peter really did not miss them. Except when the other children would ask him what he got for Christmas and he would have to tell them "nothing."

Peter was nine years old before he received his first Christmas present that he could clearly remember. Not once during his preteen years was he given the opportunity to go trick-or-treating at Halloween. He was an adolescent before he went to his first party, and he celebrated his birthday for the first time that he could remember at the age of eleven.

Early in the spring of 1958, during the Easter holidays from school, Peter was given a special treat. His mother and her new husband, Junior, took the boys with them to stay a few days. They were living in a small flat-topped house on the outskirts of the city. There was an airport nearby, and its alternating red and green runway lights would flash across the walls of the bedroom at night. Not knowing that the visit would be for only a few days, Peter was overjoyed. He thought he was going home to stay. The only thing he regretted about leaving the farm was saying good-bye to Bo. After being told for the tenth time that he could not take the animal with him, Peter resigned himself to leaving his best friend behind. Hugging the dog hard, he promised that he would come back for him when he grew up.

The trip from the Joneses' farm to their home seemed hours long. The next several days were gone almost instantly, although the family did nothing special. For Peter, just being with his mother again was enough. He seldom left her side. He would sit for hours beside her, watching television and holding firmly to her hand. Where she went, he went, not wanting to let her out of his sight. At night he would lie awake listening for the reassuring sound of her moving or talking in another part of the house until at last even his powerful determination would be overwhelmed by sleep. Occasionally he would wake up in the night, his heart pounding and body sweating with a fear he could not understand. Gripped by a nauseating anxiety, he would race to his mother's bedroom to see if she were still there. Peter would stand for long moments watching his mother sleep, cuddled close beside her husband. She would find him curled up asleep on the linoleum floor beside her bed the next morning.

After several routine days at home with his mother, Peter began to relax and feel more comfortable. He was sitting casually on the couch, picking absentmindedly at Junior's guitar that Sunday afternoon when he heard his mother sigh deeply and watched as she slowly got off the couch. He grew nervous as she began moving about the house, putting things in sacks and placing them by the front door.

Feeling as if a fever were spreading throughout his body, Peter realized that she was placing his and his brothers' things in the bags. Letting the guitar slip from his hands to the floor, Peter raced to his mother, taking one of her hands in his.

"Whatcha doin', momma?" he asked, his eyes searching hers for some denial of what was taking place.

"Junior will be home from work soon, son. We have to get ready to go," she answered, without looking into the boy's anxious eyes.

"Go where, momma, go where?" the concern in his voice made her turn away from him.

"It's time to take you boys back to the farm," she mumbled, moving quickly to the bedroom and partially closing the door.

Filled with panic, Peter sought desperately for some way to change her mind. Blaming himself bitterly for doing whatever he had done to make his mother want to send him away again, he searched the house for something he could do that would make her want to keep him with her instead. He would do anything to stay. Finally, he settled on the kitchen. His experience in the kitchen on the farm made this an easy choice. The breakfast dishes were piled unwashed on the kitchen counter.

Racing madly, he filled the sink with warm soapy water and furiously began washing the dishes. At one point his mother came to the kitchen door, stopped, and watched the desperate boy for a moment. Peter noticed that her eyes were red and puffy as he glanced eagerly at her over his shoulder.

"Look, momma, I'm washing the dishes for you!" he exclaimed. "I'm good at washing dishes, momma! You'll see. I could wash the dishes for you every time, momma. See?"

For a moment more she stood in the doorway watching the boy. Then without a word, she was gone.

Peter continued his labors. Soon the dishes were clean and piled high in the drainboard off to one side of the sink. Hurriedly he washed off the tops of the stove and counter.

He could hear more preparations for the departure being made throughout the house. Suddenly, the front door opened and Junior came in.

"Are you all ready to go?" he called out as he picked up a couple of the sacks and carried them to the car.

"Just a minute more, Junior. We're almost ready," he heard his mother answer from the bedroom.

With those words, Peter's heart sank. Beginning to sob pitifully, the heartbroken boy leaped to the cupboard for the mop. Having soaked it under the faucet in the sink, he began thrashing it wildly across the floor.

Even with tears streaming down his cheeks, Peter clung to the dim hope that if he could show his mother how much help he could be, she would not want to take him back to the farm. He poured everything he had into mopping that kitchen floor.

With eyes blurred by tears, he noticed his mother once again standing in the doorway of the kitchen.

"Momma, look! I washed the dishes and mopped the floor for you, momma! Real good. Ain't the kitchen pretty, momma? So clean and pretty? Ain't I a good boy?" the boy sobbed breathlessly as he continued flailing the mop across the floor. "Ain't I a good boy?"

Then it came. A hand on his shoulder.

"It's time to go, Peter."

"No, momma, please. Please don't make me go back, momma. I want to stay with you, momma, please!" Peter cried desperately, pulling at one of her arms with all the strength he had in his eight-year-old body.

Turning away quickly, the woman freed herself from the boy's grip and walked briskly to the door and out into the yard.

Left alone in the kitchen, Peter collapsed on top of the soggy, wet mop as he cried out his grief. For long minutes the tears came. He could not stop crying.

After awhile, Junior came into the house, picked him up, and carried him to the car. The pain in his throat and eyes began to subside. The tears slowed to a trickle and then stopped completely. The long, painful ride back to the farm began.

[Chapter Eleven]

Peter was to see his mother only one more time during the next fourteen years. The meeting occurred late in the summer of 1958.

It was Sunday. The sky was clear and the weather warm. Mrs. Jones was wearing a dress. That could mean only one thing—they were going to church.

The small Southern Baptist church was located in the village, just down the street from the school. It was an old, unpainted wooden building with a sagging roof over the porch. Its only color came from the grass and trees that surrounded it. Apart from the meeting room where the services were held, there were three smaller rooms in the back where classes could be held.

During Peter's two years on the farm, Mrs. Jones made an attempt to be regular in her attendance at the church. This was easier during the good weather months of the year when the country roads were not closed by mud or snow. For reasons of his own, Mr. Jones never accompanied them, preferring to stay at home and tend to the chores.

Dressed in blue jeans, a school shirt, and boots, the boys were ushered into the car for the five-mile ride to church. Peter didn't really care whether he went to church or not. He was quiet and shy, seldom talking or playing with other children. He would often hide from them and the adults.

The only part of the service he enjoyed was the singing. Although he never tried to join in, he loved to listen to the music director and several choir ladies lead the small congregation in the singing of old familiar gospel hymns. He particularly enjoyed watching Mrs. Jones's lower jaw quiver as she mouthed the words to the hymns. The part of the service he did not like was the sermon. He never could understand how one man could have so much to say all at once, and take so much time saying it. Peter would sit in a pew next to one of the open windows and daydream in the midst of hot summer days. Daydreaming was only one means of escape, however. Twice during his stay on the farm he actually escaped the sermon by diving headfirst out the window into the gorgeous day outside. Few people noticed these escapes because most were nodding off, trying to keep their eyes open, or sleeping in the pews. But Mrs. Jones always noticed. And a thrashing would follow in the woods behind the church after the service was over.

This particular Sunday was special. It was Homecoming, the one day a year when each family would bring food for a large picnic to be held on the grounds after church. Peter was excited. The thought of all that food, especially the desserts, made him anxious for the morning to come and go.

Driving the 1956 Chevy slowly, Mrs. Jones pulled into the graveled area precisely at 9:00 A.M. Just in time for Sunday school.

Sitting by himself in the back of the class, Peter was not the least bit interested in what was going on. All he could think about was the picnic lunch. Until the preacher and music director entered the room. Their entrance caught his·attention immediately as a hush fell across the class. The preacher had never visited their class before, so this must really be important.

Peter waited curiously. After a moment's private conversation with the teacher, the preacher turned to the class. Thirteen pairs of innocent eyes met his.

"Boys and girls," he addressed the class. "I want to ask you all a couple of very important questions. But before I do, I want all of you to bow your heads and close your eyes so that you can't see how your neighbor answers." He paused for a moment as every head bowed and every eye shut tight. "Now, then, how many of you know who Jesus Christ is? If you know who Jesus Christ is, raise your hand."

Up went Peter's hand. He could tell by the rustling of clothes and shifting in chairs that others had raised their hands too.

"Fine, fine," exclaimed the preacher. "Now, boys and girls, if you would like to know Jesus better, leave your hand up."

There was not a movement in the room.

"Praise God!" the preacher almost shouted. "The Spirit is at work in these young souls this morning!"

"Amen!" chimed in the music director emphatically.

"All right, boys and girls, you can put your hands down. Now, I want all of you who said you would like to get to know Jesus better to remain in your seats. The rest of you may be excused."

Peter did not know whether he was allowed to open his eyes or not. Afraid of doing the wrong thing, he remained where he was with his head bowed and eyes shut tight. He listened as the scraping of chairs and rustle of bodies in motion told him several of his classmates were leaving. After a moment the room was quiet again except for the buzzing of a fly nearby.

Suddenly the preacher's voice was beside him.

"You can sit up and open your eyes now, Peter."

Looking up, Peter was shocked to find that he was the only student left in the room. Even the teacher was gone. The preacher was sitting on his right and the music director on his left. They began talking to him using language that he did not understand. Such things as "eternal damnation," "Christ died for you," "forgive your sins," "washed in the blood," and "you must be saved" only frightened him. The two men were so serious. First one talking and then the other in rapid succession. All Peter could do was look back and forth, from one to the other. After a few moments, the preacher concluded.

"At the end of today's service, Peter, we are going to sing that glorious hymn of invitation, 'Just As I Am.' Now, when you hear us begin to sing that hymn, I want you to get up out of your pew, walk down to the front of the church—I'll meet you there—and in front of the whole congregation, I want you to ask to have your sins forgiven and be washed clean by the Spirit in baptism."

Without even asking if he understood, the minister stood, placed his hand roughly on the top of Peter's head, and prayed for the salvation of his soul.

Peter did not understand a word that had been said to him except that he was supposed to go to the front of the church after the service. He was scared to death.

Not knowing fully what was expected of him, Peter sat

paralyzed throughout the service, not daring to move. Not even the quiver of Mrs. Jones's chin interested him today. All he knew was that the preacher wanted him to do something important, but he did not know what it was. But he was afraid he would be in trouble and go to hell if he did not do what the preacher wanted.

Suddenly the congregation stood with open hymnbooks. The music director stood with upraised arm behind the pulpit. The preacher moved slowly down in front of the first pew. The music started. The people began to sing.

> Just as I am, without one plea,
> But that Thy blood was shed for me,
> And that Thou bidd'st me to come to Thee,
> O Lamb of God, I come! I come!

Peter was nervous and frightened. What was he supposed to do? Neither the preacher nor the music director looked at him. The second verse began. Then the third. By the fourth, both men began glancing in Peter's direction. There had been no movement out of the congregation. After verse five, the preacher stopped the music and spoke once more, inviting any lost soul to be found by Christ today. All it took was a step forward and a commitment to Jesus. Several times he looked directly at Peter as he spoke. Peter's knuckles were white as he clung to the back of the pew.

Verse six began. And ended. Still no movement out of the congregation. Again the preacher spoke, assuring the congregation that he knew for sure that there was at least one sinner, a young boy, who even at this moment stood poised to make his decision for Christ. But Satan was holding him back. After a brief prayer that the boy would be wrenched free from the grip of Satan and sin, verse six was repeated. The preacher and music director stared right at Peter. Others in the congregation noticed and turned to stare at him. Still not moving, Peter watched the scowl beginning to form across the preacher's face. Suddenly terrified, the boy found himself racing down the aisle and falling to his knees in front of the minister. Then Peter began to cry.

The minister leaned over him for a long moment waiting for Peter to ask to be saved. But the boy was too frightened to mutter a word. Standing up suddenly at the conclusion of the music, the preacher announced to the congregation that young Peter had been wrenched from Satan's power and was crying for joy in his newfound freedom in Christ, that he had asked Christ to come into his life as Lord and Savior, and that he wanted to be baptized. After a brief prayer, the congregation was dismissed. The minister had Peter stand up, smiled at him, promised to speak to the Joneses about a baptism date, and headed for the picnic.

Shaken badly by the experience, Peter hid under the first pew until the church was empty. Then moving outside, he slid unnoticed under the large dessert table covered by a large white bedsheet touching the ground on all sides. It was a perfect hiding place.

Soon the picnic began. Peter could hear the chatter of adults eating together on blankets spread under the trees. The children's laughter was further away as they continued their play, stopping only long enough to grab a chicken leg or ear of corn or piece of bread.

After awhile Peter's emotions had calmed down enough so that he felt the hunger pains in his stomach with full force. Not daring to leave the safety of his hideaway, he scooted to the back side of the table, waited until there were no shoes showing under the tablecloth, and then reached a hand out from under the tablecloth to the top of the table. Within moments he was gorged with desserts.

Suddenly Mrs. Jones's voice was beside the table.

"Young man, you get out from under that table this minute!"

Terrified once more, Peter dove for the side of the table away from that stern voice. Nearly tearing the tablecloth off with him, he made a dash for freedom around the corner, but ran full force into the preacher. Stunned, he backed away slowly, fully expecting to be struck dead by lightning at any moment.

The preacher's face was stern as he saw the several

colors of frosting smeared in globs across the boy's face. It was obvious to all what he had been doing.

Still watching the preacher, Peter was jerked away by a hand pulling on his ear, dragging him painfully through the middle of the picnicking crowd to the car. Once inside the car, Peter knew that he was in trouble. As Mrs. Jones gathered up the other two boys, Peter hurriedly wiped every shred of evidence from his face. He was so full his stomach ached and he felt nauseous.

Mrs. Jones was silent during the entire ride back to the farm. That was bad. Peter could feel the chill of his skin crawling where he knew the belt would be laid against his body. Helpless, he rode in silence like a man to his execution.

As the car topped the hill overlooking the farm, Peter was surprised and suddenly relieved to see a car parked in front of the house. That meant company. Company meant that he would not be spanked until they were gone. Hopeful once more, the boy sighed in great relief. Now he was curious about the guests.

The guests turned out to be his mother and Junior. They had driven down on the spur of the moment hoping to spend a few hours with the boys. They all piled in the car and drove deep into the river-bottom, chattering excitedly as they went. Nearing the river bridge, Junior stopped the car under the shade of a large tree beside the road. At their mother's insistence, Junior got out of the car and busied himself taking snapshots of the boys with their mother. This was the first time Peter could ever remember having his picture taken.

After a few moments, his mother turned to the boys with an announcement.

"Boys, guess what?"

Anxious and eager, the boys were all eyes and ears.

"I have a special surprise for you!" Her face was beaming with delight, her smile radiant at the expected pleasure she was about to give her sons.

"I baked it just for you boys, all by myself," she told them with a flourish as she pulled a chocolate cake and container of fruit punch from the trunk of the car.

The two younger boys cheered enthusiastically. Peter wanted to vomit. He knew that if he took one more bite of a dessert, he would most likely do just that.

Suddenly very concerned and anxious, Peter feigned surprise and excitement. Sipping the punch slowly, he held the generous slice of cake in his hand for a long moment, now knowing what to do. His mother was busy passing out slices to Junior and the boys. They began eating noisily and heartily.

Suddenly Peter hated himself for having eaten so much at the picnic. He could see how much the gift of a cake to her boys meant to his mother and how her face glowed with joy as she watched the younger boys devour their portions.He wanted so desperately to make her happy, to see her face continue to smile as it was. But he also knew the risk he took if he tried to eat it.

He looked quickly around for some place to put the cake so that she would think he had eaten his like his brothers were eating theirs. There was a large bush near the right front fender of the car. Nibbling at crumbs on the napkin, he approached the bush. The others were at the trunk of the car. With his back to them, he hoped they would not notice as he let his piece fall from the napkin into the bush.

Licking his fingers, he turned to rejoin the others. As he did, his eyes closed on those of his mother, standing halfway between himself and the other boys. She had been on her way to offer him more punch. Peter knew from the hurt and disappointment in her eyes that she had seen what he had done. She was not smiling anymore. The glow was gone from her face.

For a long, agonizing moment their eyes remained locked. The hate and bitterness for himself swelled inside the boy. He would never forgive himself for eating so much at that picnic. Even more, he knew now why nobody wanted him.

Shortly thereafter the boys were returned to the farm.

Peter would not see his mother again for fourteen years.

Three weeks later Peter was baptized during a Sunday evening service at the church. It was a big event for everyone who came. But no one paid any attention to Peter. After the service he was sent straight to the car while the refreshments were served.

After that night, Mrs. Jones never again took him to church.

[Chapter Twelve]

Christmas Eve, 1958, was an unusually warm day for that time of year. The sky was clear, the air cool and crisp. There had been feverish activity around the farm all day. Mrs. Jones relieved Peter of his cooking responsibilities and busily prepared foods of various kinds in the kitchen. The three boys had been told to stay close at hand in case they were needed. There was a strange excitement in the air that foretold the coming of an expected special event.

Early in the afternoon Peter was sitting on the front porch with Bo in his lap when he saw the strange car approaching the farm. The boy watched it come to a stop near the front gate. Hearing the car pull up, his two brothers raced around the corner of the house. While the boys remained idly where they were, the dogs eagerly greeted the visitors with curious noses and wagging tails.

After a moment a tall, dark-skinned man and two children climbed out of the car and moved cautiously among the dogs into the front yard. They stopped halfway to the house as Mrs. Jones poured out the front door, wiping her hands on an already soiled apron tied snugly around her waist.

Although he had not seen them since that night, so long ago, Peter knew who they were—his father and older brother and sister. A chill raced through his body as he watched them talking with Mrs. Jones.

Turning suddenly, Mrs. Jones called the boys to her. Afraid not to obey, the boys clustered together by her side.

"Boys, you know who this is?" she asked.

There was no answer as they stared awkwardly at the people standing before them. Peter felt a growing excitement as old memories and experiences began to resurface.

"This is your father, brother, and sister," she announced finally. The boys did not move. "I'll leave you all to visit alone. If you need anything, give me a holler. I'll be in the kitchen." She moved quickly back into the house.

Alone for the first time in three years with their father, the boys did not know what to do. They stood silently watching him. After a moment he knelt on the ground and called the younger two boys to him.

"Come here and give me a hug," he called out. David and Sharon stood behind him as the younger two bounded forward eagerly, one in each arm. Peter remained where he was. He suddenly felt a strong need to get his father's attention.

"I'm eight, almost nine," he spoke softly. Bo, at his heels, came alive at the sound of his voice, licking at his hands. His father did not hear him. Patting the dog absent-mindedly, Peter waited patiently for his turn with his father. His brothers were chattering excitedly about school, the farm, the animals, and anything else which came to mind that might hold their father's attention upon them for a moment longer. He was smiling and laughing as they talked.

Then Sharon, his nine-year-old sister, approached Peter. He watched her suspiciously. Coming to him, she wrapped her arms around him and hugged him tightly to herself.

"I've really missed you, brother Peter," she declared simply. Of all her brothers, Peter had been her favorite. She was a year old when he was born, and she had felt a special responsibility to assist her mother with his care as she grew older. Most of her free time as a child was spent entertaining him. They were constant companions, sharing childhood's many adventures and endless mysteries.

She always seemed to know when Peter was hurting or needed help. Sometimes, even in the middle of the night, she would awaken for no apparent reason and race to his crib to make sure that he was all right. She cried for days the time she had carelessly thrown the brick off the front porch, not knowing Peter was playing in the dirt beside the porch. It took eighteen stitches to close the wound in the top of his head. From that day onward Peter's welfare had been her special concern. Not that she didn't love her other brothers. She did. But Peter was special. He would always be.

All the love in her young body poured out to him. At first his body was stiff and resistant. But then the memories flooded back all at once. Wrapping his arms around her, he began to cry pitifully. The harder he tried to stop, the harder he cried. Within moments Sharon was crying too. Together they stood there alone in the middle of the yard clinging to each other, crying out each other's pain.

Their father and brothers had grown strangely silent watching them. Bo was whimpering softly, watching them with anxious and concerned eyes.

"It's OK, Peter," she would try to comfort him.

"Please don't leave me, Sissy," he would mumble between sobs.

After awhile their father stood up, putting the two younger boys down against their protest, and moved to the rear of the car.

Opening the trunk, he removed several boxes of used toys.

"Boys, these are for you. Merry Christmas!" he exclaimed, setting the boxes down in the yard.

Peter watched, still clinging to his sister, as his two younger brothers pulled the items one by one from the boxes. There was a basketball, a football, several toy guns, a well-used checker set, some old Halloween masks, and several toy cars. The boys were delighted.

During the rest of the visit Peter showed his sister all his favorite places on the farm, concluding with his and Bo's special place under the back porch. All too quickly it was time for them to leave.

They all gathered once more in the front yard to say good-bye. Peter clung so tightly to his sister that she had to fight to get away from his grasp. Having lost her again, Peter settled in the front yard with Bo in his lap, watching as the car carried her up the hill, out of sight and away from him. As with his mother, fourteen years would pass before he would see any of them again. Rocking gently back and forth with Bo hugged close to his face, Peter continued to watch the turn in the road at the top of the hill where the car had disappeared. Very softly he began singing the words to the song his mother had taught him so long ago: "Jesus loves me! this I know, For the Bible tells me so. . . ."

After the car left, Mrs. Jones came out of the house, gathered up the toys in the boxes, and carried them into the house.

"Farm boys don't need these kinds of toys" was her explanation to the boys. Within moments she had them busy with chores.

Later that afternoon, the Joneses' three adult children and their families began to arrive. Each was greeted warmly and ushered ceremoniously into the house. The boys were busy serving them drinks and snacks and bringing their luggage from the car to the house. There were five grandchildren in all. One of the families brought a Christmas tree with them. The boys were allowed to sit along the wall in the living room and watch as the grandchildren and other family members decorated the tree. Finally, packages were placed under the tree. When they asked whom the presents were for, the boys were told they were for boys and girls who had been good all the previous year. Santa Claus did not bring presents to children who had been bad.

The meal was served. Peter had never seen so much food prepared for just one meal. They were allowed to eat as much as they wanted. But unlike the rest of the family, including the children, they had to eat by themselves in the kitchen.

By the time Peter had all the dishes washed and set out to dry, it was long past sunset—his usual bedtime. He waited in the kitchen, expecting to be sent to bed. He was surprised instead when Mrs. Jones invited him and his brothers into the living room where the rest of the family was gathered around the tree and packages. Made to sit down along the wall, they were told they could stay there with the rest of the family so long as they did not get in the way.

After singing a couple of Christmas carols, the adults settled back and watched as the grandchildren began opening presents. The three boys, their eyes dancing with expectation, watched excitedly from their seats along the wall.

They watched as one present after another was opened and received enthusiastically by one or another of the grandchildren. When all the presents had been opened and several of the children asked for more, Mrs. Jones went to another part of the house and brought back the box of used toys Peter's father had left the boys that afternoon. The toys were distributed one by one to the grandchildren. Finally Mrs. Jones opened a small sack beside her chair and called Peter and his brothers to her, one by one. Each boy was given a belt and wished a Merry Christmas.

With their Christmas present clasped firmly in their grips, the boys were excused from the company and told to go to bed. Since there were so many people in the house, the boys slept on pallets of hay in the barn and used empty feed sacks for cover. When they awoke the next morning, the belts were gone.

[Chapter Thirteen]

Summers on the farm were special times for Peter. The weather fluctuated from pleasant to hot with only an occasional rainstorm to drive him inside.

Since there was no school, Peter had many long hours of free time between his morning and evening chores, free to do whatever he chose. He chose to be alone, with Bo and his brothers.

By the end of his third summer on the farm, there was not an inch of ground that he and Bo had not explored during one or another of their long walks. He knew the farm better than its owners.

Even before hearing Mr. Jones complain about the cattle escaping into the neighbor's pasture through a hole in the fence somewhere, Peter knew where the fence was down. He knew where the cows would go to have their calves in the spring and where the best place was to see deer come out of the forest to drink in the river. He knew the best trees for climbing and the best ones for bearing fruit. He knew all the shortcuts back to the house from anywhere on the farm and all the best places to cross the river. He knew the snake den, the rabbit lair, the puddle of quicksand in the marsh. There was little about the farm he did not know. It had become his own private world, a playground of sorts, a kingdom to be ruled by his fancied lordship—a home to be protected against intruders.

Ever since the visit of the school children from the city, Peter had assumed a proprietary perspective on the farm. Like Bo, it was his. All his. He wanted to keep it that way. Though he never felt at home in the house with the Joneses, he and Bo were at home in the woods. If it were not for the ever-present demands of his chores, he would never have gone into the house. He loved it outside and spent every possible minute away from the house.

By the summer of 1960, Peter's domestic duties had increased to include cooking all meals for the family, except Sunday dinner, and having full charge of the household chores. These he continued to despise.

He became more active with farm chores as well, assisting with the planting and harvesting, the bailing of hay, feeding the livestock, and dehorning and branding them. In addition, he was expected to be the primary laborer for Mrs. Jones in the family vegetable garden behind the house. In the spring, he would place a large wooden horse collar over his head, hold it at chest level, and pull the small garden plow down one row after another of unbroken soil hardened by roots and the long cold winter. Mrs. Jones would guide the plow behind him calling out, "Get up, horse!" as she snapped a small riding whip beside her. After the planting, he spent long hours in the garden hoeing and pulling weeds.

Peter worked hard on the farm. Because of his meager breakfast of two biscuits and no lunch, Peter ate heartily at supper time. Though he did not grow much in height or weight during his stay on the farm, his young body grew brown and sinewy. He became tough. The elements and hard work made him strong enough to handle most chores assigned to him.

Peter came to admire Mr. Jones. He seldom talked, but his word was law. A word from him was all it took. Even Mrs. Jones obeyed him. That impressed Peter most of all. Though he feared the man, Peter decided that he wanted to grow up to be just like him. Mr. Jones had nothing to do with the boys except when doing chores. The only conversation between them was directions on how to do this or that. Like Peter, he spent most of his time away from the house. There was very little contact between the two of them. It was almost as though Mr. Jones was not even there. Except Peter knew he was.

The greatest thrill of Peter's young life came one morning early in the fall of his third year on the farm. Peter had completed his morning chores and was about to duck out the back door before Mrs. Jones assigned him something else to do when Mr. Jones came in. After drinking his fill from the water bucket, the bronzed cowboy looked at Peter standing in fearful admiration in the corner of the kitchen.

"How old are you now, boy?" he asked.

"Ten, sir," Peter answered with a tremble in his voice.

"Reckon that's old enough," he concluded with a smile. "Time you learned to rodeo."

A light came on in Peter's eyes. Learn to rodeo! Though he had never been to one, Peter knew what a rodeo was from listening to the cowboys around the corral. It was held in the fall and every farm family in the area attended. There were bronc riding, bull riding, and calf roping; there were clowns, horses, costumes and everything! Peter was so excited he could hardly stand still. Was Mr. Jones inviting him to go?

"You wanna be a cowboy?" the man asked.

"Yes, sir, yes, sir!" Peter answered eagerly.

Mr. Jones turned from the boy and called his wife.

After a moment she appeared in the kitchen.

"What is it?" she asked as she entered. Then, seeing Peter still standing in the corner, she turned to the boy in a fit of anger. "What the hell have you done this time?"

"Calm down. The boy ain't done nothin'!" the man broke in shortly.

"Well, what is it then?"

"I'm registerin' Peter in the rodeo."

For a moment she looked at the man silently.

"To do what?" she finally asked.

"Thought he could ride old Smokey in the grand parade and compete in the calf riding. They might even have a greased pig contest this year."

For the next two weeks Peter was relieved of most of his domestic chores so that he could train for the rodeo. They were the happiest two weeks of his life on the farm. He was going to be a cowboy! Just like Mr. Jones. And ride in the rodeo yet! It was a dream come true.

For the first time Peter felt good about being on the farm, and for the first time he chose to spend his free time with adults rather than alone with Bo.

The training began by his learning to saddle and ride old Smokey, a six-year-old Shetland pony Peter had longed to ride since he first set eyes on him. The pony was gentle and easy to ride. Mr. Jones had him riding well in less than a week. Then began the more rigorous training. Several hands gathered in the corral to hold the calf steady while Peter was placed on its back. Peter would grip the halter with both hands, and the cowboys would turn the calf loose. Laughing, they would watch as the calf bucked and twisted its way around the corral trying to throw the boy off its back. Soon they began taking bets with each ride to see how long Peter could stay on.

By the middle of the next week Peter was so stiff and sore he could hardly walk. There were bruises all over his body from being thrown into the corral fence so many times.

But the boy would not give up. Gritting his teeth, he was determined to ride that calf and nothing was going to stop him. He thrilled at the attention he got from the cowboys, each trying to coach him as they perched on the top rail of the corral. Despite the physical pain, Peter loved it. He almost felt like he was one of them.

The day before the rodeo Peter found himself alone with Bo and his brothers. Everybody else was tending to chores or errands. Strutting around the barnyard like a proud rooster, Peter felt good. He really did belong. For the first time in several years he felt as if he was right where he ought to be. He never wanted to leave. It was his home.

He could hardly wait until the rodeo the following day. He would show them! They would see just how good a cowboy he really was. He was going to ride that calf, all the way to the whistle, and win that event. And how big and grown-up he would look riding old Smokey in the grand parade to start the rodeo. Everybody would see him. And everybody would know then that he was somebody!

As usual, Mrs. Jones excused the boys to go outside after their chores, warning them that they were not to set foot inside the house for any reason until time for Peter to cook supper. Obediently they deserted the house and moved toward the shade under a clump of trees to play.

As they began to get hungry that afternoon, Peter led his brothers to a large mulberry tree near the river. Climbing high into its branches, he shook the tasty berries to the ground for his brothers to eat. After about an hour, all the mulberries were gone from around where Peter was perched in the tree. He could see large, fat, juicy berries just waiting to be plucked only inches out of his reach. Peter inched his way along the branch until the berries were easily in reach. Deciding to start with those furthest away first, he reached out as far as he could. Just as his fingers closed on a choice berry, there was a "snap" and suddenly Peter was on his back on the ground looking up through the branches. His stomach hurt badly and he felt sick. As he moved to get up, he noticed his left arm lying immobile beside him. There was a large white knot at the wrist and he could not move his left hand.

He knew he was hurt seriously. Scared, he called Bobby to him and told him to run to the house as fast as he could and get Mrs. Jones. The boy disappeared in a streak.

It was a mile to the house. Thirty minutes passed before the small boy returned with a wet washcloth. Stopping at Peter's side, he handed the wet cloth to his older brother.

"Where's Mrs. Jones?" Peter asked through gritted teeth as he fought against the wave of pain sweeping through his body.

"She ain't comin'," the frightened boy answered. "But here, let me wipe your face."

"She ain't coming?" the boy cried in dismay. "Why not?"

"Peter, I'm afraid to go in the house. She told us to stay outside, remember. She might spank me!"

Peter could tell his brother was upset, torn between trying to help him and avoiding the wrath of Mrs. Jones. He knew the feeling well. For a moment he pitied his frightened, uncertain brother. Then the swelling pain made him think only of himself once more.

"It's OK, Bobby. You stay here with me," he answered. "Jimmy, I'm hurt real bad. Go wake up Mrs. Jones. Tell her I'm hurt real bad. Hurry!"

In twenty minutes Jimmy returned with Mrs. Jones. Standing the injured boy up on his feet, Mrs. Jones took his left arm in both hands, placed her foot solidly against his stomach, and pulled on the arm slowly. Just when Peter thought he could stand the pain no longer the broken bone snapped back into place and the woman turned loose. Peter collapsed on the ground, sweat and tears soaking his body.

Mrs. Jones bent down and picked up the injured boy, carrying him like a small child. She carried him the full mile to the house and laid him gently in the backseat of the car. Ordering the two younger boys into the front seat of the car, she raced to get her car keys in the house and to scribble her husband a note.

Within minutes she was speeding along the gravel roads toward town. Two miles away from town the car had a flat tire. There was no spare.

Peter was as white as a sheet, his breathing was shallow, and his stomach had become distended. In a panic, Mrs. Jones ordered the younger boys to stay with their brother in the car until she returned with help. In a run, she headed toward town.

Almost an hour passed before she returned with a man in a pickup. Removing a spare tire from the bed of the truck, he had the tire changed in five minutes. They were on their way again.

The nearest town with emergency medical facilities was thirty miles away. Driving at top speed, they were there in less than an hour. As she gently picked up the boy from the backseat of the car, Peter groaned. He could barely see her through half-closed eyes dim with shock. He caught a glimpse of people sitting around the waiting room and then of a woman in a white uniform leading them down a hallway and into a room.

As Mrs. Jones lowered him as carefully as she could onto the table, Peter passed out. Three days later he awoke to find himself in a bed in a hospital room. Mrs. Jones was sitting in a chair against the wall.

Peter had fallen almost thirty feet. He had broken his arm and sustained serious internal injuries from the fall, resulting in internal hemorrhaging. He had been unconscious for three days. The doctor told them later that Peter had missed death by a breath—a half hour later arriving at the hospital and he would have been dead.

After learning from Mrs. Jones that the rodeo had been held two days before, Peter did not care how close he had come to dying. In fact, he honestly wished that he had died.

Peter remained hospitalized for over two weeks. They were two of the most miserable weeks of his life. At his dismissal, Mrs. Jones was told that the boy was to do no strenuous labor for eight weeks and was to return to have the cast removed from his arm in ten weeks.

His dreams of becoming a cowboy and respected member of the family crushed, Peter returned to his domestic chores and hermetic life with Bo. He remained depressed for months. But at least he had Bo.

[Chapter Fourteen]

December 7, 1960. The day began like any other, except for one thing—Mrs. Jones drove Peter and his brothers to school. That was very strange because always before the boys had ridden the bus. When asked about it on their way to school, Mrs. Jones had not answered their inquiry immediately. Afraid she had not heard the question, Peter was about to ask it again when she finally answered.

"I have some business to attend to," she stated tersely.

Peter knew from experience that was the most explanation he would get. The exact nature of her business was none of his business. His curiosity was roused even more, however, when she parked the car in the small parking lot behind the high school building and walked toward the principal's office after sending them off to their respective classrooms. Something was not right. Peter could feel it. The thought worried him until the demands of classroom performance commanded his full attention.

Peter was now ten years old, soon to be eleven. He had been on the farm over three years. It had been two years since he had heard from or seen any of his family. He had all but given up ever seeing them again—with one exception. His sister. He had promised himself two years ago, when he last saw her, that he would live long enough to find her. Since the accident, Peter had withdrawn from adults once again, feeling like a total failure. His world consisted of his brothers, the farm, Bo, and now his driving desire to be reunited with his sister. They became his only reasons for being alive.

He had performed well in school. Now in Mr. Davis's fifth- and sixth- grade class, Peter was always top of the class in academic performance. He had made only one friend in the school. Delsey was a tall, half-retarded girl crippled by polio in her youth. She had flunked three years and was a social outcast in the school due to her disfigured body and slurred speech. She was the only child with whom Peter felt comfortable—all the others avoided him because he avoided them.

Peter and Delsey had first become friends after the beauty contest in the third grade. She had been one of the last three girls left standing in front of the class after the voting, as Peter had been among the boys. A couple of days after that event, afraid that it might happen again and convinced that he was as ugly as she, Peter had approached Delsey and struck a deal with her. He promised to vote for her as the prettiest and most well-groomed girl in the class next time if she would cast her vote for him. That way, they each would have one vote.

Though the contest was never repeated, their agreement became a bond of friendship between them. Despite the catcalls and ridicule of the other students, the two "rejects" became good and close friends. They walked the playground together, ate lunch together alone at one end of the long tables in the rear of the cafeteria, and sat near each other on the bus. Peter even tried to help with her schoolwork, mouthing the answers to oral questions given her during drills, doing her homework for her, and even designing cheat sheets she could pin on the inside of her sweater neckline and cuffs during exams. In opposition to all others, they drew closer and closer together until they were almost brother and sister. He spent long hours telling her about Bo and the farm and all the things he liked best. She had cried when he told her about his mother. She wanted his mother to come back and take him home. She told him how her parents made her hide in the cellar when company came so that no one would see her and laugh at her. One time she stayed there a full weekend without food or water. She did not mind it too much though, she said, because she had imaginary friends who lived there with her. They were her friends because they liked her. And how lucky she was, she said, that he liked her too.

Around 10:00 on that frosty winter morning, December 7, 1960, Mr. Adams, the school principal, entered the back door of the classroom. The class was silent except for the muffled sounds of pages turning and pencils scratching across paper. The air was heavy with concentration. As one, Mr. Davis and the entire class of students turned to see who had entered. Peter, too, was curious about what business would bring the principal into the classroom. It must be very important indeed.

"I'm sorry to disturb your class, Mr. Davis," he said apologetically.

"That is quite all right, Mr. Adams. Please come in. What may we do for you?" Mr. Davis seemed as curious as were the students.

"Mr. Davis, I have come for Peter. Please collect his personal things for him. We will send for his records later," the principal announced softly, looking toward the surprised boy.

The class let out a gasp of surprise and wonder as all eyes turned to watch Peter. What had he done? Was he in trouble? Where was Mr. Adams going to take him? Peter was suddenly frightened. Memories of other sudden and unexplained moves leaped into his mind.

"Is everything all right, Mr. Adams?" asked the bewildered teacher.

"Please, Mr. Davis. Just do as I asked. I'll explain later," the principal cut him short.

In a matter of minutes his pencil, notebooks, erasers, and crayons were collected into a small brown paper bag. Taking them slowly from the outstretched hand of his teacher, Peter searched his face for some explanation of what was happening to him. There was nothing there but concern. He became even more frightened.

"Come with me, please, Peter," Mr. Adams called from the rear of the class. "Class, tell Peter good-bye."

Peter was so stunned and frightened he could barely move. Good-bye? Where was he going? What was happening to him? His body began to tremble as the uneasy feeling in his stomach twisted into a hard knot. Slowly, he eased out of his desk, where only a few short minutes ago he had been buried deeply in a reading assignment, oblivious to the world around him. Peter watched the principal's face for some sign of anger, or unhappiness, or displeasure that would explain why he was being removed from the class. But he found no anger or displeasure. Only sadness.

Peter stopped for a moment at Delsey's desk. Her eyes were wide and frightened. He could think of nothing to say to her, his best human friend. Reaching into his pocket, Peter pulled out the lucky rabbit foot he had found on the playground and handed it to her.

"Here, Delsey, I don't need it no more," he said as she took it in her crippled hand, and began to cry.

Peter thought for a minute Mr. Adams was going to pick him up and hug him. But he didn't. Instead, he looked at the frightened boy, took his hand, and pulled him gently out of the classroom, through the restroom and lounge area that separated the three classrooms, and on through the third- and fourth- grade class taught by Mrs. Adams.

Everyone watched as they moved down the aisle toward the back door. Several of the students waved as he passed. Peter looked for his two younger brothers, but they were already gone. With tears beginning to flood his eyes, he turned to look at Mrs. Adams as they neared the door leading out of the building.

"Good-bye, Peter," she said softly, looking away.

Something terrible was happening to him. He did not know what. But he knew that once again his life was about to be turned upside down. And he was scared to death.

Mr. Adams wordlessly walked the boy to the cafeteria, a building which was between the high-school and grade-school complex and easily accessible to each.

As they entered, Peter was struck by its familiar sights, sounds, and smells. Long wooden tables with wooden folding chairs on all sides. The tray line and all the kitchen equipment behind that. The cafeteria ladies, as they were called affectionately, all dressed in white aprons were busy preparing lunch. It all seemed normal, except for one thing. It was not time for lunch. No children were there.

Mr. Adams took Peter to a table where his two younger brothers were sitting. He asked him to sit down. Mrs. Jones was standing in front of them across the table. Without a word, Mr. Adams left.

Dressed as he remembered her that morning, Mrs. Jones looked at them a long moment before speaking. All three boys sat quietly waiting, afraid to talk or move.

"Boys," she began. "Boys, do you remember me telling you that the day may come when you might be taken from me, when you might have to go live with someone else?"

"Yes, ma'am," they answered in unison, each beginning to sob. Already Peter knew. Like so many times before, they were being moved to another home, another family.

Peter did not hear any more of what she said. He did not even ask why. After three years with the Joneses on their farm, he was being moved once again.

After awhile Mrs. Jones took the boys outside and placed

them in the backseat of the car. She said she had to speak with the principal and would be back shortly.

Sitting there alone with his two younger brothers, Peter pulled out a piece of paper and his crayons. Drawing carefully, he colored a picture of the American flag he could see waving freely in the breeze from the playground flagpole. It included stripes and stars. He still has that picture, even today.

The five-mile drive into the western countryside to the farm seemed very short. What used to be so familiar now seemed strange, as though he had never really seen it before. In no time they were there. The sheriff's patrol car was already parked at the front of the house. There were three small cardboard boxes sitting on the front porch.

"You boys can wait out here if you want, or come inside with me," declared Mrs. Jones as she entered the house.

Without a word the three boys sat down on the steps leading up to the porch and cradled their chins in the palms of their hands. Peter sat with his brothers for a few minutes, then got up and moved dejectedly to the backyard in search of Bo. Oh, how he loved that dog. From the first day he arrived on that farm until now, Bo had been his constant companion. Romping in the early morning through the woods, watching sunrises from his treetop perch, going about the farm doing his daily chores, tumbling topsy-turvy in a heap of frolicking boy and dog, even sleeping together on the same large tuft of grass under the back porch, they were inseparable. Not once had the dog ever growled at him or barked at him or bitten him. Bo was always there, eager to be with him and glad to see him. Peter was sure the dog loved him as much as he loved the dog.

Peter found Bo huddled against the cold under the back porch. When Peter called softly to him, Bo crawled out from under the porch, stretched, and then, with his tail wagging fiercely, hurried to Peter.

Peter sat on the grass with the dog cradled in his lap, his head pressed hard against his face. Once again the words to the song his mother had taught him so long ago came suddenly to the boy's lips, his childish voice singing them the only way he knew how:

> Jesus loves me! this I know,
> For the Bible tells me so. . . .

Over and over again he sang those lines, holding Bo tight and rocking back and forth. Then the call came. It was time to go.

Peter gave the dog one last hug, got up slowly, and then kicked the bewildered animal as hard as he could in the ribs before he ran sobbing to the open door of the sheriff's car waiting to take him far away, never to come back.

That morning life had been routine. The sun had risen, as usual, on that farm. But somehow, sometime during that day the course of the sun had been changed so that Peter could no longer be sure where it would set. But even more frightening for Peter was not knowing where to look tomorrow morning in order to see it rise again. Even though he had hoped it would be different this time, that they might be able to stay and not be taken away, somewhere in the back of his mind Peter was expecting it, sensing that it would only be a matter of time. After all, who really wanted three boys that nobody wanted? After all, he was ugly, no one liked him, except Delsey and Bo, and he was so bad that not even his mother and father wanted him. How could he expect anyone else to want him?

It was noon by the time the sheriff's patrol car pulled into the parking lot of the Palomino Motel in the city. The drive from the farm had been quiet and uneventful.

The boys were left sitting in the backseat of the car while the deputy sheriff and welfare worker went to room number thirteen and knocked on the door. Almost immediately the door opened and the two men disappeared inside. Minutes passed. Finally, the door opened again. The deputy sheriff came to the car. Reluctantly the boys moved from the car and entered the motel room.

"Boys," announced the welfare worker as they entered, "these are your new parents."

There was a young couple standing beside the welfare worker. Reaching out, they each shook the boys' hands in turn. About all Peter could remember of either was that they seemed tall and both were wearing knee-length trench coats. Nothing else attracted his attention.

After a moment of staring, each boy was offered a small cap gun with an accompanying roll of caps, and they were asked to wait out in the parking lot. Sitting down on the edge of the sidewalk, the boys began firing their cap guns.

It was not long before the four adults came out of the room. The three small cardboard boxes were removed from the trunk of the sheriff's car and placed in the trunk of the other car. Then the deputy and welfare worker were gone.

[PART III]
The Adoptive Home

* * * *

Peter was almost eleven years old when he was adopted. During the five years since the breakup of his family he suffered heavy personal losses. Not only did he lose his father and older brother and sister, but he lost his mother three times. As a result of these losses and welfare department intervention on his behalf, Peter had to adjust to, and cope with, many different mother figures, an equal number of residential environments, frequent school changes, and the intermittent separations from his younger brothers—all in the course of five years.

One of the keys to human survival is the ability of the individual to cope with change. The emotional and psychological health of even the most mature, well-adjusted adult would be challenged severely by such radical, frequent changes in so short a time. Children are even more vulnerable because they lack the psychological resources for coping with change that come from experience.

The initial loss of his family was severe enough for Peter. The subsequent movement from one foster home to another, combined with the sporadic visits and departures of his parents, only perpetuated and intensified that loss. His grieving was never allowed to terminate, being constantly renewed and deepened by treasured, hopeful moments with loved ones that always ended in good-byes.

Initially the intervention of the State Child Welfare

Department on Peter's behalf was a therapeutic success. It provided him a place to live and assured him the basic necessities of life. Few would argue, however, that in the long run, therapeutic intervention in Peter's case was a dismal failure. The treatment applied only increased his suffering, resulting in cumulative trauma which, itself, became life- and health-threatening. It is not enough simply to meet the physical needs of such a child. Psychological, social, and developmental needs also must be met if the health and welfare of the child are to be maintained. Failure to do so is like a physician treating the external, visible wounds of an automobile accident victim while ignoring the possibility that the victim is bleeding to death internally.

By the age of eleven, Peter's world consisted primarily of other children, places, adults, and animals. Animals he loved. Other children, apart from his brothers, he envied and ignored. They were different. No, he was different. A freak maybe, or a mistake that never should have happened; a quirk of nature that had no place in the natural flow of life and families. He constantly was reminded in countless nonverbal ways that he was a child no one really wanted.

Places he loved. The world was his playground. The forests, rocks, ravines, trees, sunrises, rivers, and ponds, all were his to enjoy. He loved being outside with Bo. He belonged in the forest. It was his home. Places never changed. They remain the same day after day. His special tree near the river was always there and welcomed him without a sound into its branches. He never could get lost in the forest because the paths were always there—as much a part of the forest as the trees. Nature was permanent. Only its appearance would change from season to season. The things that mattered stayed the same. Especially the sunrises. He could count on them.

Adults frightened him; yet Peter yearned for them to be a part of his life. He needed desperately what they had to offer. Yet his survival depended on avoiding what they gave. Adults were not to be trusted. They only brought pain.

By the time he was adopted, Peter had resigned himself to never having a permanent home, never being like other children who were loved and wanted, never being good enough. He felt he would be always on the move, hungry, frightened, and alone. He was convinced that there was something terribly wrong with him that made him unlovable.

He had learned that relationships were transient things, providing warmth and nourishment for a time, and then gone abruptly, leaving an even greater emptiness in their wake. Love was something you took wherever you could find it—take it and run, because inevitably it would evaporate. Relationships were to be avoided if he was to survive. They always hurt. Too much sometimes.

Peter took three years to adjust to farm life, but it took less than a minute—just one word, "good-bye"—to take it all away. With one swift move everything about his life changed. The Joneses were gone. The farm was gone. The school. The church. Delsey. The security of his routine chores. His walks in the forest. His tree. The river. And Bo. All were gone. Stolen away from him as effortlessly as a hunter's bullet steals the life from its unsuspecting prey. Nothing remained but memories. Memories as real, as painful, and as fading as yesterday.

Different faces, different places, different rules and expectations. From farm life to city life. From farmhand to dependent child. From wide open spaces to fenced-in backyards. Paths through the forest to paved city streets and sidewalks. From Bo to no one. Dream turned nightmare.

Everything was different and strange. Everything except those old familiar feelings of being unloved and unwanted. They never changed.

[Chapter Fifteen]

The first three weeks with his new adoptive parents were all but lost to Peter. He was sure they would soon realize the mistake they had made by adopting him, recognizing him for what he really was—bad and unlovable. Then they, too, would send him away. He believed his stay with them was only temporary. He made no effort to interact with the family. Unless told to do something, he would sit mute and alone on the living room couch for hours, staring blindly out the window. Day after day he remained buried under a heavy depression and showed no interest or concern for anything happening around him, deaf and oblivious to everything. Not even his brothers could stir his interest. The boy did not care anymore. Nothing mattered. All he wanted was to be left alone. Totally.

His mind was filled with memories turned horror stories. He would remember schoolbus rides through the countryside when children were dropped off at their homes. Then at a particularly sharp curve on the mountain road, and when only he was left on the bus, his mind would let the bus miss the turn and tumble headlong down the side of the mountain to the rocky ravine far below. Or a time wading the river with Bo. Instead of jumping across from one large rock to another, he would miss his mark and plunge into the fast-moving waters of the river. Its pull would drag him deeper and deeper, away from the light on the surface into its dark, gloomy depths. Or that harmless snake he found in the chicken house that time would suddenly become a diamondback rattler with fangs buried deep into his outstretched hand. Peter felt a sense of pleasure at these fancied attempts at self-destruction. He replayed them over and over, savoring the power he felt and the joy of their promised finality. One after another the destructive fantasies paraded before his mind's eye, becoming more real than the strange faces of his adoptive parents which came occasionally to stare into his.

His adoptive parents tried everything they could think of

to get the boy to talk and open up. Nothing worked. He drew deeper into himself, closing out the world around him.

Then one day it happened. Peter's adoptive father came home for lunch. It had been raining. Mud from the edge of his boots smeared on the carpet as he entered the front door. Peter's new mother was busy moving bowls of steaming soup and sandwiches from the kitchen to the dining room table. After all was ready, she called for the boys to come to lunch. The younger two were there instantly, but Peter did not hear the call.

When she went into the living room to call Peter once again, she noticed the mud on the carpet. A housekeeping perfectionist, she let fly the rage which swelled inside her as she raced toward Peter still sitting on the couch. Her fury startled the boy. Slapping his face, she dragged him by the hair from the couch and slammed his head hard against the front door. Crying in panic, Peter slumped to the floor as she kicked him hard in the stomach.

"You smeared this mud on the carpet, didn't you, you little bastard?" she screamed, still in a rage.

She had the boy's full attention.

"No, ma'am, I didn't . . ." His answer was cut short by her foot driving deep into his stomach once more. Fighting to regain his breath, the boy gasped out frightened and painful sobs.

"You lying ———," she exploded at him. With eyes blazing fiercely and teeth grating, the frenzied woman grabbed the boy's face in both of her hands, digging her fingernails into the skin around his eyes, nose, and cheeks. "You are lying to me, aren't you, Peter? You did bring that mud into the house, didn't you?" The boy was sobbing hard from the pain in his stomach and face. "Didn't you? Answer me, damn you!" she roared, slapping him so hard on the mouth that blood began to trickle from his lips.

Peter tried once more to deny her charge. But the rage that poured out upon him convinced him that he had better agree to whatever she said.

"Didn't you, Peter?" she was still screaming.

"Yes ma'am," the terrified boy answered.

Slowly her rage slipped away. Turning loose of the boy's face and neck, she moved back a step, still glaring fiercely at him. Her voice was harsh and bitter.

"You lying piece of scum. I wouldn't have had to spank you if you hadn't lied to me, now would I?"

"No ma'am."

"It's your own damn fault, isn't it?"

"Yes, ma'am."

"And you did track the mud in, didn't you?"

"Yes, ma'am."

"And you can talk, can't you?"

"Yes, ma'am."

"Well, let me tell you something, little man. Don't you ever, ever lie to me. I'll tear you apart, do you hear me?"

"Yes, ma'am."

"And when someone talks to you, you answer them."

"Yes, ma'am."

"And I am fed up with you sitting on that couch pouting all day. Do you hear me? I don't care whether you wanted to be adopted or not, you were, and you damn well better like it! You got that?"

"Yes, ma'am."

There was a long pause as the woman stared hard at the frightened boy. She had finally gotten through to him after all.

"Bill and I take you three boys into our lives to give you a good home and what the hell thanks do we get? Not a damn thing! You better shape up, buddy boy, and I mean now! I want to see a smile on that pouty mouth of yours and I want some happy cooperation around here. Do you hear me? Happy cooperation. That's what I want, and by damn, that's what I am going to get!"

"Yes, ma'am, " Peter mumbled, trying hard to smile through swollen lips.

"All right. You go wash your face and then get your butt back in here and you pick up every piece of mud out of that carpet. And don't you move until it is spotless. Do you understand me?"

"Yes, ma'am," the boy answered as he raced off to do as ordered. After a moment he returned to the living room. Dropping to his knees, he began digging at the mud smeared on the carpet.

After a moment of watching the boy's efforts, the angry woman moved to the table where her husband and the two younger boys were already seated. Her husband said nothing as she sat down. Jimmy and Bobby were pale and frightened, their eyes wide with fear and concern for their brother.

"I think I found the way to get his attention. What do you think?" she asked casually as the meal began and ended without Peter.

"Yes, I believe you have," her husband answered as they continued to watch Peter dig hopelessly at the mud-smeared carpet. "I do believe you have."

[Chapter Sixteen]

Peter's adoptive father, Bill, worked as a research engineer for a large construction company in their western home town. Some time after the adoption he was transferred to a coastal city. Though he had completed only two years of college, he prided himself on the professional level he had achieved in the company and community while competing with more educated and younger men. He even held several patents through the company. A large, stocky man, he stood six feet tall, with thick, broad shoulders and muscled arms. He was a veteran of the Korean conflict and countless battles fought in his younger years across one football field after another throughout the state. After seven years of childless marriage to Judy, he had agreed to adoption.

Judy was the last of thirteen children born to her family. She was raised in hard times and poverty. By her own strength and ingenuity she graduated from high school and then worked her way through a two-year training program to become a licensed practical nurse. She had taken a leave of absence to spend some time at home with her new family. She was an attractive woman, tall and full-figured. In her lighter moods she could be warm, friendly, and charming.

To all who knew them, Bill and Judy were a model couple, happily married, successful, and affluent. They were involved in the community. They attended church regularly and were involved in its many activities. They were well liked and respected. No one doubted they would make ideal parents for three homeless boys.

In the days that followed the incident of mud on the carpet, Peter became hyper-alert to the wants and desires of his adoptive parents. He knew what had happened to him that day could happen again. He did not blame his mother for losing her temper and hurting him. After all, it only confirmed what he already believed about himself— that he was bad and deserved punishment. He tried to atone for his evilness by catering to their every wish, bringing them coffee in bed, preparing dinner, running errands, doing anything to try to get them to like him and not hurt him again. He believed that he had made them unhappy enough to beat him. It was his responsibility, therefore, to make them happy enough not to need to beat him.

The harder he worked, the less he pleased them. Blaming himself, Peter would push to do more. The more he did for them, the more they expected and demanded of him. Whatever he did was never enough. They always seemed to expect more. Or, what he did was not done well enough.

Unlike on the farm, Peter could not get very far away from them. His freedom was limited to the house and small yard surrounding it. There was no place to hide, no place to escape their almost constant surveillance. He was forced by his setting to interact with them. His instinct for survival, heightened by the threat of physical violence against him, drove him endlessly to find ways to please them. But try as he might, every attempt was a failure because every attempt was criticized as inadequate, inappropriate, or simply insubordinate. His battle to please his adoptive parents was lost before it began.

One morning his mother woke up complaining of menstrual cramps. She was in a terrible mood. Nothing Peter did could please her. Everything was wrong. Over and over again that day she berated and criticized him, telling him again and again how incompetent he was in every activity he attempted. By afternoon he felt miserable. Obviously his mother was unhappy again. And it was his fault. He did not know exactly what it was that he had done, but he had done something to make her unhappy. He was sure of that. Besides, she would not have cursed at him the way she did and called him those awful names if it was not all true; if he was not really a bad person.

Feeling depressed and guilty for making his adoptive mother so unhappy, the boy wandered aimlessly around the front yard lost in his own thoughts. Suddenly he noticed the dandelions growing in the grass, their bright sunny colors standing out clearly from the carpet of green around them. He was struck by how fragile and beautiful they were. Looking at them reminded him of the endless days on the farm when he wandered the fields and forests, both constantly alive with wildflowers, and how he enjoyed stopping to smell them and stare amazed at their complex designs and infinite colors. It made him feel good to remember his walks in the woods with Bo. Dropping to his knees, Peter gently picked a handful of the dandelions, being especially careful not to mash them or bend any of their stems. They reminded him of the sunrise he would watch from the top of his tree. Suddenly the boy felt better and decided to take the bouquet to his mother as a gift. Maybe the beautiful flowers would make her feel better.

He just knew that she would smile and be happy when he showed them to her.

Easing himself quietly into the house through the front door, Peter tiptoed to the dining room table where she sat writing a letter.

"Mama?" he spoke softly, his voice barely able to hide his excitement. Though he hated to call her "mama," that was what she expected and so he complied. The word no longer carried any meaning for him.

"What is it, Peter?" she answered sternly, not looking up.

"I brought you something, something special. See!" He thrust the bouquet of flowers out in front of him toward her, smiling with expected pleasure.

Looking up, the woman stared at the flowers for a moment. Then her face began to turn red and her jaw clamped shut. Jerking the flowers from his hand, she threw them viciously to the floor.

"You damn little brown-nosing ————!" she screeched at the boy. "How dare you bring me a bunch of weeds! Now get the hell out of my sight."

Crushed and terrified, the boy moved quickly to do as she commanded. He could not understand what he had done wrong. Somehow or other he had made her unhappy again. And she called the flowers "weeds."

Feeling worse than before, Peter hid himself from her the rest of the afternoon. He was afraid he would make her angry enough to hurt him again.

When dinner was served that evening, Peter responded hesitantly to the call to the table. With great reluctance, he joined the rest of the family at the table. He was still upset about what had happened that afternoon. He was not the least bit hungry. Besides, his parents were not talking. Instead, a heavy silence hung in the room. That could mean only one thing—trouble. He was tense, nervous, and wary as he took his place.

After the blessing was barked out by his father, the dishes were passed—each to the right. Although Peter did not want anything to eat, he took generous portions of each food item because he knew they would be unhappy with him if he did not. They might even get angry.

Within moments his mother noticed that he was only nibbling at his food.

"Don't you like my cooking?" she demanded threateningly.

"Oh, yes, ma'am. It's delicious. It's the best I've ever eaten!" he exclaimed anxiously.

"Then eat it!"

"Yes, ma'am!"

Peter began eating a little faster. He felt upset at his stomach and nauseous. He was only half through by the time his parents were finished. Not a word had been said through the entire meal. Jimmy and Bobby ate quietly, afraid of what was about to happen.

Peter paused for a moment trying to let the food settle before forcing down another bite. Slowly he traced a flower on his plate.

Suddenly a pair of knuckles slammed down hard on the top of his head. He began to cry as his head filled with pain.

"Your mother told you to eat, young man." It was the hard voice of his father for the first time.

"Yes, sir!" screeched the now terrified boy through stifled sobs and a spoon of food plunging into his mouth.

"Here! You want to be stubborn. I can be stubborn too," his mother declared firmly as she emptied the remaining contents of every dish into his plate. Then taking her fork, she mixed all the food together in a slop on the plate. Next, she took his glass of milk and poured it over the pile of food. "Now, eat it all. Now!"

"Yes, ma'am."

Peter began cramming forkful after forkful of food into his mouth as fast as he could, hardly taking time to chew before swallowing. They watched his every bite, amused.

"Well, look at the little pig eat!" exclaimed his mother. "I guess he was hungry after all, wasn't he, daddy?"

"Looks that way."

"Hey, hold on a second," she ordered. Peter stopped eating, watching her cautiously. "Let's do this right. If he wants to eat like a pig, why not let him be a pig?"

Taking the dish from the table, she placed it in the middle of the kitchen floor.

"Come here, little piggy," she called Peter to her. "Now get down on your hands and knees and put your nose in the dish and eat like a little piggy."

The frightened boy did as commanded. On hands and knees he began lapping at the slop on the dish like a dog. His stomach hurt. With every bite he felt more sick. His parents stood in the hallway laughing at him.

Suddenly Peter heaved. He fought to keep the food in his stomach.

"Damn you! Don't you dare throw up on my kitchen floor, Peter! Peter! Do you hear?" screamed the woman at him.

Then it came. All the food he had been forced to eat came right back up and spilled across the kitchen floor. Peter began crying hysterically.

The now furious woman grabbed Peter's head by the hair and began pushing his face through the vomit on the floor.

"Eat it! Eat it, you bastard," she was screaming. "How dare you disobey me!"

Two hours later it was all over. After mopping the floor with his face and hair, Peter was forced to stand in a corner of the kitchen while being interrogated by the two angry adults. They blocked any possible avenue of escape. They wanted to know why he had disobeyed his mother's command not to vomit. They accused him of lying when he answered that he could not help it, that he had really tried not to throw up. Angry again, they beat him with their fists until he admitted that he had disobeyed on purpose to get even with his mother for not accepting the weeds.

As punishment for disobeying and lying, Peter was given twenty licks with a belt across the back of his legs. Numb with pain and misery, the boy was then made to clean up the mess on the kitchen floor, take a bath, and go to bed. His stomach and legs hurt so badly he could hardly walk. But he made it. He did what they told him to do. The pain in his face and head throbbed mercilessly as he lowered it gently on the pillow. Sleep could not come fast enough.

[Chapter Seventeen]

After weeks of feeling helpless and frustrated in their relationship with Peter, his adoptive parents had now found a method of motivating and controlling his behavior that seemed effective and gave them a genuine sense of power and control over Peter, and his brothers as well. The younger boys were scared. So far only Peter had experienced the full punishment of their wrath. But watching him suffer made the other two aware of their own helpless vulnerability. Their days suddenly became filled with one ambition—pleasing their new parents. If they could somehow do enough, maybe they would be spared. A rivalry among the boys began, each trying to outdo the other in a battle to win the approval of their parents. A word from either adult expressing any need would send the boys racing and pushing against each other in an attempt to be the first one to bring the cup of coffee, glass of water, or whatever.

If either of the younger boys made a mistake, Peter was often blamed. His parents became convinced that he was trying to stay between them and the younger boys, to protect them, and to lead them in a "conspiracy" against their authority and control. The bond between the brothers was stronger than any possible bond between parent and child, and they resented this. As a result, Peter was beaten many times for being the "ringleader" when one of his brothers transgressed or became the target of parental displeasure. He was blamed for everything. It was true that the boys had a close bond between them. Having experienced so much hardship together, they were all but inseparable. For years Peter had served in a surrogate parental role, caring constantly for his brothers and their welfare. They continued to look to him for basic want and need satisfaction.

Bill and Judy noticed this quickly and did all in their power over the years the boys lived with them to break Peter away from his brothers. They tried to get the boys to hate one another, to turn on each other in their own fight to survive. They would make the younger boys sit in Peter's lap and kiss him on the mouth, hug him and run their fingers through his hair, and fondle his genitals. In an attempt to give his parents what they were looking for, Peter would push his brothers forcefully from his lap onto the floor in a show of disgust. Although he knew the falls hurt, he also knew that they hurt his brothers a great deal less than the beatings they would receive if they did not do as commanded or if he failed to convince his parents that he was sincere in his disgust. He hated them for forcing him to hurt his brothers.

In other attempts to break the bond between the boys, the adults would make the younger boys team up against Peter with belts and fists—trying to get the younger boys to see Peter as they saw him, as a threat in need of punishing. Peter was beaten constantly for things he did not do. At those times his parents would lavish large amounts of attention and special privileges on the younger boys and make Peter sit and watch—hoping to turn them against each other. He would be made to do his brothers' chores, serve them their meals, work as their personal slave. The adults would spend hours talking to the younger boys about how "sick" and "bad" Peter was, trying to convince them to turn against their older brother because he was not to be trusted. The younger boys were required to report Peter's every move. If Peter did something "wrong," they would be beaten if they did not report it.

When Peter's parents spoke to him, they always pointed out how bad, how stupid, or how ugly he was. Never was he hugged, held in their lap, or kissed good night. He was like an enemy to them living under the same roof or like a limb grafted onto their body which they rejected by cutting off the flow of any life-sustaining nourishment in the hopes that the unwanted limb would die, rot, and fall off. The intensity of the abuse was almost as though they were in a fight against evil, where only the most determined and severe means would bring them victory. It was almost as though they were defending themselves by beating Peter. No matter what he did, it was wrong. Countless hours of leisure family time were spent either beating Peter or mercilessly assaulting him verbally. His abuse became the family pasttime, even the family obsession.

After awhile their only ambition toward Peter was to "break" him as a cowboy would break a wild horse. They spent long hours planning and designing new ways to inflict pain.

Late in the first year of his stay in the adoptive family, Peter was given a lesson in obedience he would never forget. It was late. Peter lay deathly still on the bed buried in the illusion of safety within the cocoon of blanket pulled far over his head. He knew from experience that once his parents had gone to bed he would be safe until morning.

Late at night was the only time he felt safe. Every other hour of the day he was alert to an attack by his parents at any time from any place for any reason. He spent his days at home trying to be inconspicuous, trying not to draw his parents' attention, but to blend in with the woodwork and furniture. He was seldom successful. He treasured the night hours. Many nights he tried desperately to stay awake all night so as not to miss one precious second of its solitude and peace. He would even count seconds, hoping that the passing of the night would seem slower and the dawning of morning would be delayed. There was protection in darkness. Morning only brought exposure.

This night was no different. But his parents had not gone to bed yet. He was still in danger. Try as he might to escape and deny the brutal nightmare taking shape around him by taking refuge in his private world of fantasy, he had to keep his ear tuned to those murmuring voices in the other room that usually brought him pain.

In a way, the sound of his parents' voices was comforting—in the same way that the rattle of a snake nearby is comforting compared to the deadly silence that follows. As long as the voices continued, he was fairly safe. But when they stopped, one of two things would happen. They would either go to bed or they would come for him. It had happened so many times before, just that way.

The voices suddenly stopped. Tense and alert like a terrified animal in a trap, Peter tuned his every sense to the silence that now bombarded him as he probed the unknown beyond his bedroom walls.

There was no movement, no sound. Only that awful, agonizing silence. Maybe they would go on to bed this time. Please, dear God, just this once.

Clinging desperately to that one dim hope, the boy waited breathlessly. A lifetime of seconds passed. And then it came. Footsteps. Outside his bedroom door. They were coming for him.

With eyes shut tightly in despair, Peter strained hard against the mattress that would not absorb him.

There was nothing he could do to prevent what was about to happen to him. Whimpering quietly, the boy began urinating uncontrollably as the bedroom door burst open.

Almost before he knew it, Peter had his only blanket of protection jerked forcefully from his grasp and the hard, cruel hand of his father wrapped itself around his ear, pulling him painfully out of the bed and into the blinding light of the living room.

Infuriated at the sight of the wet pajama bottoms clinging to the boy's small frame, his father released the now bleeding ear and smashed a fist hard against the side of his head, sending him sprawling into the furniture lining the wall.

Paralyzed with fear, Peter lay motionless on the floor

where he had fallen until his father's hard-soled boot slammed hard against his buttocks with the order to stand up.

Scrambling to do as commanded, Peter felt his soggy pajama bottoms slip from his waist and fall in a pile around his ankles, leaving him standing naked in the middle of the room.

Amused, the boy's parents sat down on the couch opposite him. For long moments they stared at him in silence, their eyes cold, calculating, and merciless. Peter dared not move, even to pull up his pajamas.

Then he noticed the all-too-familiar array of belts, hoses, and switches neatly arranged on the carpet beside the couch. As the full impact of his desperate situation burst upon him, the boy lost control and began crying hysterically.

A slashing diamond ring tearing at the side of his face sent the boy sprawling on the floor once more. He was forbidden to cry. He knew that—from past encounters with his parents. His crying, they said, was only his infantile attempt to get them to feel sorry for him. His "refusal" to stand up and take his "medicine" like a man only infuriated them the more. Fighting frantically to regain control of the emotion that would not be tolerated, Peter again responded to the command to stand up.

The weight of his parents' judgment descended upon him. In a voice that would echo throughout the rest of his life, Peter was told that the time had come for him to learn what it means to obey an order. And it was their duty as parents to see that he learned just that.

The naked boy was made to stand as high up on his tiptoes as possible with his hands clasped together as far above his head as they would reach. In that position he was ordered to take one blow from his father's belt across his bare stomach without showing any physical or emotional reaction whatsoever. He was not to move and he was not to cry out. The blows would continue until the order was obeyed.

An hour and a half later the badly beaten boy collapsed unconscious in the middle of the floor. Over thirty blows with a belt and long rubber hose had been dealt to the stomach and groin area of his body, which by then was a black, swollen mass of bleeding flesh, torn and hanging loose in places. There were welts and bruises on his shoulders, back, and legs. The bottoms of both feet were bleeding, having been switched unmercifully by his enraged mother while his father held him pinned to the floor.

When Peter awoke the next morning, he could hardly move. The pain was still almost as great as when the blows were pounding out scars on his body. His stomach was so swollen that he had to hold it up with his hands to keep it from sagging and bouncing when he moved. His raw feet began to bleed again when he tried to walk. Although he had been forced to bathe in a cold salt bath before finally being allowed to escape into sleep, he awakened to find that the wounds all over his body had wept so badly during the night that the sheet upon which he lay and the pajama bottoms had dried to his body, forming scabs through the material. In a show of mercy, Peter's parents allowed him a lukewarm bath in order to soak the sheet and pajama bottoms off rather than having them pulled off forcefully as they threatened to do.

Peter missed a week of school while his body healed. He spent most of his time at home hiding from his mother. Though he was in desperate need of bed rest, he was expected to continue his chores.

Eventually his body healed. His heart and his mind never did.

[Chapter Eighteen]

The boys were entered into school shortly after arriving in their adoptive home. It was a small suburban grade school within easy walking distance of their house. Peter was placed in the fifth grade.

Once a week each class had a library period during which the students were introduced to many kinds of literature in the hopes of inspiring them to read. The essentials of education were reading, writing, and arithmetic, the students were told over and over again.

Although Peter knew how to read, he had no real interest in reading. It was just something you had to do in school. Until one day when the class was given a free reading period in the library. Every student was expected to read something of his or her own choice.

As usual Peter sat by himself in a corner of the library classroom. As the other children moved about the rows and stacks of literature in search of a book that would attract and hold their attention, Peter sat where he was as though he did not know what to do.

The librarian, a small elderly woman, watched him for a moment before moving to his side. She was struck by his appearance of helplessness. He seemed painfully timid, almost as though he was afraid to get up and go about his chore without specific instructions from his teacher.

"Peter?" she called, as she neared the boy.

The boy jumped at the sound of her voice near him. There was a strange fear in his eyes as he turned quickly in her direction.

"Yes, ma'am?" he answered quickly.

"Oh, Peter, I'm sorry! I didn't mean to startle you!" she spoke softly, trying to calm the nervous boy. She watched as the pupils of his eyes slowly returned to their normal size. "Can't you find a book to read, Peter?" she asked finally.

Suddenly the boy was frightened again. Was he doing something he wasn't supposed to be doing? Maybe he had done something wrong. He did not know what to answer the woman. It did not occur to him that all she wanted to know was whether or not he had found a book to read.

"Peter, for heaven's sake!" exclaimed the librarian as

she watched him emotionally cowering away from her. "You haven't done anything wrong, son. Don't be afraid like that. You're really not in trouble! Come on, let me help you find a book!"

The woman took Peter's hand and pulled him passively among the shelves of books. Several times she stopped to browse among the titles. Finally she withdrew a book and handed it to him.

"What do you think about this one, Peter?" she asked.

Peter took the book into his hands and stared at the title and jacket cover. The picture was of two boys standing in a cave around a large chest of gold. The picture caught his imagination. It looked interesting.

Seeing his obvious interest, the librarian pushed him toward a reading table.

"Now, Peter, I want you to read at least one chapter today. If you like the story, then you can check the book out and take it home to read. If you don't, then we'll just keep looking until we find one you like. OK?"

"Yes, ma'am."

As the librarian moved away, Peter opened the book and began to read. Slowly at first, but then faster. As the characters and story began to unfold, Peter hungrily sought out every detail, every word. He was soon caught up in the story. Not wanting to leave the story, Peter was both surprised and disappointed when the librarian suddenly announced the end of their library period. He wanted to continue reading. Closing the book reluctantly, Peter checked the book out and carried it with him to his next class.

The story of the two boys trying to solve the mystery of the hidden treasure so intrigued Peter that he returned to it every time he had a spare moment during that day. By noon the following day he had read the entire book. When he returned it to the library during his lunch break, he got up enough courage to ask the librarian if she had any more books like that one. As luck would have it, that book was one in a series of fifty adventure thrillers about these same boys. By the time he graduated from fifth grade, Peter had read all fifty of them and had turned to other adventure series as well.

Peter became an avid reader and spent every spare moment reading. He became the characters he read about and lived their adventures.

Apart from reading, his time at school was the only other escape he had from the horror of home life. As the beatings became increasingly more brutal and frequent, Peter sought out reasons to stay at school. Although he did not particularly like sports, he tried to play everything he could so that he could stay a few hours after school for practice. He also tried to join clubs or to volunteer to stay after school to help the teacher clean up the classroom. Anything that would delay his having to go home.

Peter dreaded the afternoon. He would begin watching the clock during his homeroom period after lunch. Hardly a minute would pass without his noticing its passing. He was just one more minute closer to having to go home. His tension and anxiety would build until, by the time his last class of the day was dismissed, he would be a nervous wreck. He hated three o'clock and would have done anything to avoid having to go home.

He never knew what mood he would find his mother in when he opened the front door. Once in a while she would be engaged in some activity around the house and pay him no attention. On those occasions he would sigh in deep relief, change his clothes quickly, and lose himself in the book he was reading at the time. But that was rare.

Most of the time she would put him to work immediately on some household chore. But it was never enough that he do the chore. It had to be done perfectly. It was never done well enough to suit her, however, no matter how hard he tried. She always found something wrong with whatever he did.

One afternoon she put him to work cleaning the bathroom. After he worked meticulously for two hours, she came in to inspect his work. Peter was nervous and apprehensive as she checked the bathtub, the sink, mirror, walls, floor, and toilet. There she stopped.

Lowering the lid of the commode, she noticed that he had neglected to clean behind it. The truth of the matter was that he had cleaned behind the lid. But the cleaning rag she had given him to use was ragged and had left a string and some lint on the porcelain surface. Suddenly in a rage she accused Peter of not having cleaned the bathroom at all. When he assured her that he had cleaned everything in the room, including the commode, she grabbed his head by the hair and pushed it hard against the tank behind the lid so that he could see the "filth" he had left behind.

With his mother screaming into his ear and pounding his head against the tank, Peter finally admitted that he had not cleaned the bathroom as he said he did. He had lied. He was trying to get even with her. That was what he knew she wanted to hear. Nothing else would do. The truth did not matter. His only chance was to tell her what she wanted to hear.

After his confession, his mother very nearly drowned him in the commode. Over and over again she slammed his head against the bottom of the toilet, his face totally submerged in the water. By the time she quit, the water was red with blood pouring from his nose and Peter was gasping desperately for air, coughing and choking on the water already in his mouth and lungs.

Peter was ordered to clean the bathroom once again. He spent the rest of the afternoon in the bathroom, cleaning it over and over again, polishing everything until every fixture looked like a mirror. Even though the room was spotless, Peter knew he could not stop cleaning until his mother gave him permission to do so. On and on he went, cleaning and recleaning, polishing and repolishing.

Finally his father came home from work. His parents came together to the bathroom where Peter was on his hands and knees scrubbing the floor for the sixth time. His mother made him stand up and tell his father what he had done. The boy had to tell his father that he had disobeyed his mother and had lied to her, that he was rebellious, and that he deserved to be punished. The bruises already on the boy's face and neck went unnoticed. The only thing that seemed to matter to him was that his wife was upset.

In a fit of rage, the angry man grabbed the plastic bag his wife held in her hands. It was a bag she used to store vegetables in the refrigerator. She was folding it to put away in the kitchen when he had entered the house. Taking the bag, he pulled it over the boy's head and held it tightly around Peter's neck.

As the air inside the bag grew thin, Peter panicked. Thrashing wildly, he clawed at the hands holding the bag tightly around his neck. The bag tore loose as his father's fist exploded into his face and sent him crashing into the bathtub. Peter paid no attention to the blood streaming from his nose once again as his lungs sucked in great breaths of air. But the relief was only temporary.

Furious that he would attempt to free himself, his father jerked him to his feet. Pulling Peter's arms straight out behind his back, he pressed his knee into the lower part of the boy's back, while his wife put the bag over the boy's head once more. Holding it tightly around his throat, she watched as his face turned blue.

The last thing Peter saw before losing consciousness was his mother's face pressed very near his own. It was filled with anger and hatred.

[Chapter Nineteen]

Peter's obedience training continued. Again it was late. Peter and his brothers were huddled in their beds. Again his father came for him. But this time he called to Peter from the bedroom door.

"Peter, come with me."

An icy chill raced through his body as he fought back the

panic these words caused. Moving quickly to do as commanded, Peter stumbled his way into the living room. His father reclaimed his seat in a recliner next to the wall. His mother was sitting in a padded rocking chair beside him, smoking a cigarette. They were separated by a table floor lamp.

"Yes, sir?" the boy responded, his squeaky voice barely audible through a constricted throat.

They sat silently staring at him for a long time. The only sound was the occasional inhaling and exhaling of smoke from their lungs.

Peter dared not look away from them for fear of being accused of ignoring them. The penalty for such an offense was severe. But neither did he dare continue to look at them for fear of being accused of trying to stare them down. The penalty for that was equally severe. Crying was out of the question. That would only infuriate them. If he dared to speak up, he would be charged with arrogance and disrespect. He did not know what to do. A nervous sweat covered his body. He could hardly stand still. The sudden need to urinate made him even more uncomfortable. But he dared not move. It was an agonizingly familiar position in which even the most innocently assertive action could be interpreted as a threat and used as justification for punishment. It was a no-win situation, specifically designed to be just that. It would be hell if he did or hell if he didn't. Pure hell. All he could do was wait and suffer.

Peter was so tense and frightened by all the things that they might do to him that he did not comprehend what his mother said when she finally broke the silence, speaking in a whisper.

"Sit down."

"I beg your pardon?" the anxious boy answered.

"Don't you dare stand there and disobey me and pretend you didn't hear me," the woman screamed at him. "Now you had better do what I told you to do and I mean now!"

"Yes, ma'am!" Peter was terrified. He could kill himself for not hearing what she had said. If only he had been listening more closely. He did not know what the woman wanted him to do.

"Do it, Peter! Now, damn you."

"Yes, ma'am, yes, ma'am!" he was frantic. Dancing nervously, he looked desperately for some clue of what she had told him to do. He knew that if he did not do something immediately, he would be beaten for disobedience.

Seeing the empty coffee cups sitting on the table between them, he took a chance that she had ordered him to bring her more coffee.

As he sprang toward the coffee cups, his father's fist met him squarely on the jaw, sending him sprawling on the floor.

"Damn you, boy! You trying to play games with me?" he demanded fiercely.

"No, sir. Honest I'm not!" the boy pleaded desperately.

"You're a damn liar!" cut in his mother. "You know damn good and well what I told you to do, don't you?"

Again Peter was trapped. If he answered no to her question he would be beaten for lying. But if he answered yes, then he would be beaten for willful disobedience. It was hopeless. Either way he answered, he was in trouble. And that could result in only one thing. Another beating.

After only a brief moment, his mind quit trying to find a way to avoid what he knew was inevitable. He was going to be beaten again. There was nothing he could do or say to stop it. In complete dismay, he resigned himself to it and tried as best he could to prepare his mind and body for the pain soon to come.

"Peter, so help me God, if you value your life you had better answer me, and right now." His mother's voice was vicious.

"Yes, ma'am," Peter answered, his voice flat and emotionless. He fixed his eyes on a spot on the table and withdrew deeply into himself.

"Yes, m'am, what?" her voice demanded.

"Yes, ma'am, I did."

"Yes, ma'am, you did what?" the angry voice continued.

"Look at me when I talk to you!"

"Yes, ma'am." Peter turned his empty eyes to her and fixed them on a spot between her eyes.

"Yes, ma'am, you did what?" she demanded once again.

"Yes, ma'am, I did hear what you said."

"You cocky, arrogant bastard! Why in the hell I ever adopted you I'll never know. You are nothing but scum—filthy, slimy scum. You don't even deserve to be alive. Why don't you just die?"

Peter stood motionless before them. Curling her lips in a snarl, the woman cleared her throat and spit full into the boy's face. The sputum slid down the length of his face. Peter made no effort to remove it.

After a moment of staring at him in disgust, she turned and addressed her husband who was sitting back in his chair and glaring savagely at the boy.

"Well, daddy, it looks like this stupid ——— didn't learn a damn thing the other night, doesn't it?"

"Looks that way."

"What do you suppose it's going to take to teach him not to lie?"

"Damned if I know. A damn mule has more smarts than him. Guess cutting out his tongue would cure him of lying, don't you think?"

"That it might, that it might. Want me to get a knife?"

"Not necessary. I've got one right here," he answered, pulling a large knife from his pocket. "Come here, boy."

Peter thought he was going to pass out. He moved hesitantly to the spot where his father pointed beside his chair.

"Now stick out your lyin' tongue and hold it out. And don't you dare move!" the man ordered.

Peter was terrified. With his right hand he held out his tongue as far as he could. He watched the blade of his father's pocketknife as it came to rest on his tongue. Glancing up, he saw his father's eyes boring viciously into his own. Suddenly the blade began to move across his tongue. The pain shot into his mouth, making the boy jerk away. As his mouth filled with blood, he heard his father's voice, cold and mean.

"You just refuse to obey, don't you, big man? You think you can just do anything you damn well please. Well, buddy boy, I've got news for you. Now get back up here, and I mean now."

Peter hurried to do as commanded. He watched in frozen terror as his father readied the knife once more. As he turned again with the knife to the frightened boy standing helplessly by his chair, his wife cut in.

"Oh, come here, baby. Are we being mean to our poor baby?" she whined in a voice intended only to mock. "Come here and give mama a hug. Mama loves you so much. She'll kiss it and make it all better."

Peter moved toward her, trying to give her a hug as she had demanded. As he drew near, she smashed her fist hard against his chest, sending him falling onto the floor.

"Oh, I'm so sorry, my poor baby. Come here and give mama a big hug. Tell mama you love her now."

Peter got up painfully, tears flooding his eyes once again, and tried to obey. For an hour they made the helpless boy go back and forth between them as they taunted him with a constant barrage of verbal abuse. Each time he was made to tell them he loved them and offer them a hug. Each time he was knocked down by a blow to the chest or stomach. And they would laugh at him for being stupid enough to keep coming back for more in obedience to their commands. Once Peter just lay where he had fallen on the floor, ignoring the next command and hoping that maybe it would stop if he showed them he was smart enough to know that it was a game they were playing with him. Instead, they beat him for being disobedient. The game continued. The laughter and ridicule hurt as bad as the blows. By the time they tired of their sport, Peter's chest was black and blue, his ribs and stomach ached from bruises, and his tongue was so swollen he could hardly talk.

The ordeal continued the following afternoon. Bringing

him again into the living room, his parents outlined the rules of the new game.

"Now, Peter," his mother began, "I know as well as I know that I am sitting here in this chair that you heard what I told you to do last night. You are being deliberately stubborn and disobedient. Now, if we have to stay up all day and all night, we will. But for once in your miserable life you are going to be honest and obey. You, buddy boy, are going to obey my command and do as I told you or you are going to be one sorry _____!"

Peter stood silently in the face of her challenge. Just as he had been all the other times and the night before, he was trapped. He had no idea what it was she wanted him to do. His fear began to swell into panic.

"Now, son, what did I tell you to do?" she asked softly.

Desperately, the boy sought the answer she wanted to hear. He could think of nothing.

"I don't know," he mumbled, knowing that it was the wrong thing to say, but knowing equally well that he had to say something.

"You don't know or you don't remember?"

"I don't remember."

"You don't remember," she smirked. "Well, maybe we can help you remember." After thinking a moment she continued, "How much money do you have saved up?"

Peter had worked during his lunch period in the cafeteria as a dishwasher all through junior high school. He had earned one dollar per hour and had saved every penny. He was planning to use the money in an escape attempt. It was his key to freedom. Stunned by her question, the boy felt overwhelmed with despair. Now they were going to take his money away from him too. There was no hope.

"Four hundred and eighty-four dollars and seventy-six cents," he answered softly.

"Four hundred and eighty-four dollars and seventy-six cents," she repeated. "And how long have you been saving it?"

"Since I was in seventh grade."

"It must be pretty important to you."

"Yes, ma'am."

"Good. Maybe keeping it will provide enough motivation for you to tell the truth," she smiled. "Here's what we are going to do. It is going to cost you one dollar for every second it takes you to tell me what I told you to do and to do it. Starting right now," she concluded, turning her eyes to her watch.

"One dollar. Five dollars. Ten dollars," she called out the passing of seconds in a monotone.

Frantically Peter sought the solution to his dilemma. That money was very important to him and was slipping quickly away. He *had* to come up with the right answer.

"Fifteen dollars. Twenty dollars," the voice droned on.

"You told me not to lie?" he guessed.

"Wrong," his father answered.

"Thirty dollars."

"You told me to obey?"

"Wrong."

"Forty dollars."

"Clean up the kitchen?"

"Wrong."

"Wash the dishes?"

"Wrong."

"One hundred dollars."

"Bring you coffee."

"Wrong."

Peter danced nervously from foot to foot. He was distraught in his race against time.

"You told me to straighten up?" he asked hopefully.

"Wrong. You're playing games, buddy boy. You're only hurting yourself," his father answered.

"One hundred and fifty dollars."

"Happy cooperation?"

"Wrong!"

"Go to bed?"

"Go to hell."

"Two hundred dollars."

Almost half his money was gone. Under the pressure, Peter could not think of anything else.

"Two hundred and fifty dollars."

"You better quit stalling," his father cautioned.

Peter broke. Collapsing in a heap on the floor at their feet, he cried hysterically. On and on he cried. All the pressure, terror, and frustration could no longer be held in check. It all came out at once. It was hopeless. His money was gone. All that hard work and saving, for nothing. Everything was gone. And he could do nothing to stop it.

"Three hundred and fifty dollars."

The seconds ticked away. His misery and despair deepened into life-wrenching sobs. He could not stop.

"Four hundred dollars. Four hundred and eighty-four dollars and seventy-six cents. Well, that's it," she announced with a smile. "Guess we are four hundred and eighty dollars richer, daddy."

"Yep, guess so. He's a stubborn one, isn't he?"

"Yeah, but it cost him!" she smiled. Turning back to Peter, she spoke to the anguished boy still crying hopelessly on the floor. "You can quit putting on a show now. We're not impressed. Get your butt up and go get our money."

Peter obeyed mechanically. His desperation eased somewhat and his crying stopped. He went to his bedroom and brought back the coffee can stuffed with dollar bills and loose change. Handing them his key to freedom, the boy was suddenly filled with rage. Turning his eyes away so that they would not see the hatred there, he fought against the urge to go berserk. In his mind he could visualize his hands around her neck, squeezing slowly, tighter and tighter, squeezing until her face turned into a twisted mask of black death. He watched joyfully the pain streaking across her face as the blood and oxygen supply gradually diminished; he took great satisfaction in her screams for mercy. He thrilled at the thought. Lost in these pleasurable thoughts, Peter had not noticed the long silence in the room. His adoptive parents were staring at him curiously.

"Get the hell out of my sight before I puke all over you," his mother shouted. "I can't stand the sight of you."

Peter disappeared in his room for the rest of the afternoon. Sure that a beating was yet to come, he tried desperately to lose himself in his latest book.

Suddenly the call to supper came. "Boys, wash up!"

His anxiety mounting, Peter raced to the bathroom to wash his hands. As he applied a generous lather to his hands, his brothers came running in from the backyard, swarming into the bathroom with him. Jimmy closed the door so that he could urinate.

Before he could finish, his mother jerked the bathroom door open and shouted for the boys to get out of the bathroom. They raced headlong into the dining room.

"Peter, why did you call your brothers into the bathroom? A little family conference maybe? Starting up a little conspiracy?" she demanded fiercely.

"No, ma'am! I was just washing my hands and they . . ."

"You lying bastard!" she screamed, cutting him short. "You know damn good and well that you called them in there and closed the door so that we wouldn't know what was said."

She slapped him hard on the face.

"Now I want to know what was going on in there! Now!"

"Nothing . . . ," the boy tried to answer.

"All right then! If you weren't trying to stir up a little rebellion, then you were masturbating! Which was it?"

Again Peter was forced to admit to something he had not done. After several vicious licks from a rubber hose across his buttocks and the backs of his legs, he admitted to masturbating.

With the boy's confession made, his father was satisfied and he laid the rubber hose aside. But his mother became more furious.

"All right, you perverted piece of scum, you want to masturbate in front of your brothers, you get right up here on this chair and masturbate in front of the whole damn family," she shouted as she tore off the boy's clothes.

Totally nude, Peter was made to stand on a chair in the middle of the room and masturbate himself while his mother ridiculed him. His impotence infuriated her more.

She screamed as she grabbed hold of the boy's penis and began jerking him violently. When he still did not get hard, she tried to tear the organ from his body, pulling him painfully around the room.

Finally she released the crying boy and his father took over.

"Get up against that wall, damn you!" he shouted. He had been watching in silence.

His father made him spread apart his legs and arms and then lean his weight on his hands against the wall and on the balls of his feet. For a while it was a welcome relief from the pain he had just experienced. But then the muscles in his arms and legs began to ache.

Every time he came down off the balls of his feet he was beaten. All evening long his parents sat and watched him. All evening long he stayed in that spread-eagled position against the wall, high on his tiptoes.

The pain was excruciating. Three times his legs gave way and he fell to the floor. Each time he was beaten with a rubber hose and made to resume the position.

After many hours he collapsed and could no longer stand up. He had no control of the muscles in his arms and legs. No matter how much they beat him, he could not stand up.

Dragging him by a leg, his father threw him painfully across the bed. In only a moment Peter was asleep. But before he was, the boy had just enough time to pray that he would never wake up.

[Chapter Twenty]

But Peter did awaken. From that living nightmare and every one that followed. For two weeks afterwards he was beaten morning and evening routinely. Ten licks with the rubber hose. Not because he had done anything deserving punishment. On general principles, they told him. He was bad. Or so they told him and so he believed.

Peter was forced to live with his adoptive family for almost seven years. From December 1960 until the summer of 1967. It was seven years of pure hell. Not a day passed unnoticed by Peter, each filled with actual or threatened physical and emotional abuse. Although he yearned for the day when he would be old enough and strong enough to escape from them forever, he welcomed the passage of each day and dreaded the coming of the next.

He spent his adolescent years trying to survive the mental and physical tortures imposed upon him by his parents. All seven years were filled with terror. The threat of beatings was ever present. His every move was scrutinized and judged as a possible justification for abuse. Their only reason for treating him so brutally, they told him, was to make a "decent" human being out of him. Because he was so stubborn and rebellious, less severe methods, they said, would not work. They had no choice but to "paddle" him. They really did not want to. In fact, they declared that it always hurt them more than it did him. They just did not know how to teach him in a few years what he should have been taught in eighteen. His natural parents and the foster homes had twisted his mind and screwed him up, they said. They loved him enough to try to straighten him out while there was still time.

He tried to run away many times. Running away from home became his only way to postpone a beating. Each time he hoped that no one would find him. But each time the police would pick him up wandering alone on the empty streets at night and take him to juvenile authorities. There he would be placed in temporary custody until his parents could be notified to come and get him. They always came. And the delayed punishment always was administered.

On one occasion Peter refused to go home with his parents. The juvenile guards dragged him into the shower room and made him dress in his street clothes. When their backs turned for a moment, Peter began banging his head as hard as he could against the tiled wall, hoping to hurt himself badly enough to require hospitalization. The guards stopped him before he could accomplish his goal. Forcing him out of the shower room, they sat him in an interview room with one of the guards blocking the door and watching him closely. Before long, a woman entered the room with the other guard.

She introduced herself to Peter as a psychiatric social worker employed by the state at that institution to help young people like him work through their problems. She wanted to know if Peter would tell her what was bothering him so that she could help him.

Peter had never talked to an adult before about what was happening to him at home. He did not trust them. But he was desperate. Maybe she would help. Maybe she could make them not send him back to his parents.

For an hour Peter talked while she listened. He told her everything. Occasionally she would ask questions and make notes in a file in front of her.

When Peter finished, she smiled warmly and assured him that his parents had no intentions of hurting him and that everything would be all right if he would only try harder to get along with them. Then she left the room.

A moment later the guards were back. Each grabbing an arm, they dragged Peter into the family waiting room where his parents sat, looking concerned.

On the ride home, his parents laughed at what the psychiatric social worker had said. Apparently she had suggested strongly to them that he needed P.T.—psychiatric treatment—in order to relieve him of fantasies of persecution. In summary, his parents promised him P.T. But not psychiatric treatment. Physical treatment. Peter was beaten for his efforts to seek rescue.

Never again did he trust an adult enough to reveal what was happening to him. His parents threatened to kill him if he did. Even worse, the disbelief of the social worker only confirmed what the boy already knew was true—no one would help him because he was bad and deserved the punishment he received. It was all his fault. Why else would the very people who were supposed to love him the most, his parents, beat him?

This belief was reinforced repeatedly during those seven years. Why did not the neighbors, who surely must have heard the screams in the middle of the night, do something to help him? Or the relatives who actually witnessed several of the beatings? Their only response was to tell his parents that some day Peter was going to kill them while they were asleep in their bed. Such comments only brought him more misery and hardship. Why did not the police suspect something when he ran away from home so many times? Or his teachers at school? Surely they must have wondered at the terror in his eyes, his reluctance to go home, and the bruises on his hands and face. They were all silent. And Peter suffered in silence, believing that it was all his fault for being bad.

Though his parents attended church religiously, even singing in the choir, Peter found little comfort there except that the threat of beating was temporarily removed. But that was enough for him to want to be there as much as possible. He grew to love going to church and he often would sit amidst its dimly lighted emptiness through the entire coffee hour until time to go home.

Any attempt to reach out to his parents or brothers was seen as an aggressive gesture and was rejected or punished immediately. Soon he quit trying. His world became himself, his reading, and school. Nothing else was possible. Nothing else mattered.

Mealtimes were the most dangerous times for him. Daily he was forced to sit totally exposed and vulnerable to his parents. Most other times during the day he could manage to remain out of their immediate range of vision. To draw attention to himself was to invite punishment. To avoid contact with his parents was an important survival technique.

He had no control of mealtimes though. He was forced to be present. The table conversation more often than not focused on him. It was almost always critical and punishing. He was reminded over and over again that he had no right to one bite of the food being forced down his throat. He had no right to anything they were providing him—clothes, shelter, food. He had no right to be there. Only out of the goodness of their hearts did they allow him to stay in the home. Peter believed them.

Peter believed all of this and more. He was convinced that it was his fault his parents had to beat him. The only feelings he had for himself were shame and guilt—shame for being what he was, a dependent, bad child, and guilt for being alive.

Many methods of inflicting pain were used on Peter. Some of these were beatings with belts, hoses, switches, boards, and leather straps. Burns from open flames, hot baths, and matches and cigarettes were not unusual. Slapping, hitting, kicking, twisting limbs, pinching, and biting were common techniques. Sticks, rocks, and bricks also were used. After a couple of years his parents would sit around the dinner table in his presence, planning new methods and designing new instruments that would inflict greater pain than their usual procedures.

One night at dinner his mother beat the top of his head into a soft mush with a knife handle because she believed he had lied to her. Again and again the knife handle crashed against his skull. With each blow of metal on bone, Peter's head would explode with pain so severe it temporarily blinded him. His ears rang with pain. Within an hour after the beating, a large black mass formed under the skin on his head and began moving slowly down his forehead. Both eyes soon swelled shut. The black mass moved the length of his face and came to rest in the tissue under his chin. For several days afterward his face remained blackened as the drooping mass under his chin began to dissipate. Peter had severe headaches for weeks afterwards. His parents never knew it.

The emotional abuse inflicted upon the boy was equally severe. He was incessantly belittled, criticized, and shamed. He was told constantly how bad he was. He knew his parents hated him. But he was sure it was his fault. There was nothing secure or predictable about his world at home. Almost every day was filled with tension, anxiety, and fear. He existed in a world which he preceived to be hostile and extremely dangerous. Everything became threatening. Even his own need to go to the bathroom. After he went to bed at night, his need to urinate would drive him almost into a panic because to do so would require his getting up, opening the bedroom door, and moving where they could see him down the hall to the bathroom. Such visibility might catch their attention, and his presence out of bed after bedtime was cause for punishment. He functioned at a level of simple survival. Every thought and action was in service of that one essential goal.

Peter learned to trust no one, to keep a constant vigilance for impending violence and danger, and to become hyper-alert to the slightest changes in mood, posture, or vocal tones of his parents. Most of his energy and effort at home was spent trying to avoid contact with them, to predict their every want and need, to supply that need, or to fulfill their performance expectations of him regarding his chores and other assignments. The only semblance of security and peace he had was in sleep and while at school. But even that was tenuous due to the unpredictable nature of his parents in their relationship with him. He did not feel safe anywhere at any time.

The worst times were when they would tie him to a chair and make him watch and listen as they beat his younger brothers, all the while telling them it was Peter's fault they were being beaten. His brothers would scream for Peter to help them as their bodies were being bloodied. On the foster farm Peter was able to watch out for his brothers. He took care of them, even taking their spankings for them. Always before he could help them with almost any need. Now, suddenly, he was totally helpless. Their screams to him for help and his inability to do anything drove him nearly out of his mind. To this day Peter is not rid of those horrible screams. The scenes play endlessly before his mind's eye; the pitiful screams remain a constant reminder of the hell out of which he grew.

During 1967, his junior year of high school, Peter had a temporary job working as a busboy in a downtown restaurant on weekends. He valued the job highly because it kept him away from home most of the day on his scheduled work days. His parents would not allow him to have a car nor was he permitted to have a driver's license. As a result, he had to walk to and from work. It was approximately eight miles from his home to the restaurant. On most days he would have to leave home before sunup in order to get to work on time. And there were many days in which he did not return home until after sundown. He worked as many hours as his employers allowed him. He did not mind. In fact, he wanted it that way. Although he feared his employer's authority, he did not fear being beaten while on the job. That was a tremendous relief. Twice he physically collapsed on the job because he was too sick with fever to work but refused to tell anyone or to stay home.

His route to and from work would take him past the church. Many times he would stop on his journey home and enter the empty church. It was so quiet and peaceful. And so beautiful. It came to represent for him everything good and beautiful about life and people. Peter loved those times in the church, although he never once really felt alone there. He always felt as though he was sitting in the company of someone, in the presence of something good, something powerful and gentle. It had a beckoning quality that made it hard for him to leave and eager to return. Somehow or other the pain and agony of everything that had happened to him did not matter there. It was as though they were left behind—out there somewhere—having no place of power in his life while he was there in the midst of the enveloping warmth of presence.

Like the tree on the farm, the church became his special place. A place of refuge, comfort, and security. He felt warm, secure, and accepted in the midst of the immutables. It became a home he treasured. He did not like it as much when the people were there. He liked it best when he was alone in the presence of whatever power inspired its peace and beauty.

During the summer, Peter had a difference of opinion with his employer and his parents told him to walk off the job. He did—and lost one avenue of escape.

Late that summer his parents decided to take a vacation. They were to be gone two weeks. Peter and his brothers were left at home.

It was a Friday night. With his parents gone, Peter had disregarded his household chores. The entire house was a mess: dirty dishes everywhere, clothes lying around, ashtrays full of cigarette butts, beds unmade, and bathrooms uncleaned. The irresponsibility after so many years of heavy performance demands felt good. Besides, his parents were not due back from vacation until Sunday. That was day after tomorrow. He planned on spending all day Saturday getting the house cleaned and back in order before their arrival home.

He was half asleep on the couch when the front door suddenly opened. It was his parents. They had decided to come home early to catch him in the act, as they told him. Their eyes hungrily surveyed the scene. They did not miss a detail. Peter knew he was in trouble—big trouble. Dreadful chills raced through his body.

Angrily his parents confronted him. Their words were harsh and bitter. He knew they were justified. The dirty house only confirmed what they and he believed—that he was worthless and bad.

As the verbal barrage slackened, they told him they were

going out for dinner but they would return in an hour. If the house was not as it should be by then, they were going to stomp a mud hole out of him.

It was an impossible assignment. Even as the door slammed shut behind them, Peter knew there was no way he could have everything the way they would want it in just one hour. But he knew he had to try. He also knew he deserved whatever treatment came his way. He began racing madly about, cleaning the house.

The hour passed in what seemed like ten minutes. He was dripping with sweat and breathing hard. Feverishly he was pushing the vacuum across the living room carpet when the front door opened and they came in again. He had only completed the kitchen, living room, and den. The upstairs rooms were still untouched.

He froze at the sight of them. Without a word they glanced through the downstairs rooms and moved past him on their way upstairs. For a moment Peter breathed a sigh of relief. Not a moment later, however, their bedroom door burst open and his mother raced down the hall and stairs, shrieking his name. Grabbing him by the throat, she shook the frightened boy furiously while screaming incoherently in his face.

After a moment his father freed her hands from Peter's aching neck and hit him hard on the side of the head. Peter stumbled against the wall but did not fall.

An hour passed before Peter realized what specifically had triggered their rage. As his parents entered their bedroom, his mother had noticed that the mattress on the bed was slightly overhanging the box springs on one side. In her mind this could only mean one thing—Peter had been sleeping with some girl in her bedroom and on her bed. Nothing could have been further from the truth.

Peter's denials were useless and only perpetuated their fury against him, resulting in escalated brutality. He knew that he could be hurt seriously if he did not confess and tell them what they wanted to hear. He might be hurt badly anyway, but he had a better chance if he confessed.

Finally he told them exactly what they wanted to hear. For a moment their rage abated.

But then it swelled up again. Grabbing the boy by the neck, his father threw him out the front door. He tumbled headlong down the concrete steps leading away from the porch and came to rest in a pile on the lower sidewalk at the edge of night's eternal darkness. As he lay stunned, he could feel the large bump begin to swell on the back of his head.

Glancing toward the front door of the house to see if they were coming after him, Peter saw the figures of his parents silhouetted against the light in the living room. In voices filled with disgust and scorn, they spoke their last words to him.

"Get the hell out of our sight. You don't belong here. You never did. You belong with the slime on the streets. And, by God, don't you dare ever try to set foot in this house again!"

The darkness engulfed him as the door slammed shut forever. At long last, the holocaust came to an end. Peter was free but terribly alone. Free and alone to make his way as best he could in a world where he did not belong. Free and alone at last to find his mother and sister, to begin his desperate search for the love he deserved and needed but never had. His search for a mother's love and acceptance continues into this present day. A lonely, endless search whose object and time no longer exist.

[PART IV]
On His Own

* * * *

Peter was almost eighteen when the ties with his adoptive family were severed. The years since the breakup of his biological family had been harsh, difficult ones.

Already a troubled child by the age of six, he had his problems compounded by the foster home experiences. The stress and anxiety of dealing with his perpetual grief, coupled with the almost constant need to adapt to changing life conditions, took a heavy physical and emotional toll. After almost five years in the foster home circuit, Peter was not a good candidate for adoption. There was no clinical reason to believe that an adoptive home placement would be any more successful than the foster homes. In addition, his adoptive parents had no idea what they were getting in Peter and his brothers. They were not prepared to deal with troubled children.

During the abusive years in the adoptive home, Peter functioned at a level of survival. Nothing else mattered. His daily struggle to survive preempted most other activities normal for his age group. He was able to function successfully in school due to his natural ability. In all other areas he was delayed developmentally. Socially he was retarded.

The emotional and behavioral adaptations which were necessary for survival in the home were totally inappropriate outside the home. They only provided a barrier between himself and other people, heightening his own sense of inadequacy and estrangement. Believing himself at fault, deserving the rejection, punishment and abuse, Peter was a deeply disturbed young man let loose upon the streets. He had nothing going for him but his rage and desire to survive.

[Chapter Twenty-one]

A pair of blue jeans, a white T-shirt, tennis shoes, and thirty-five cents. With these resources Peter began his new life alone.

For hours that night Peter wandered the empty streets, more alone than he had ever been in his life. Everything important and familiar was lost. As it had many times before, the entire setting of his life changed in an instant. Everything that had been a part of the scene a moment ago was gone suddenly. Familiar things were replaced by a heavy darkness that offered only its cold and uncertainty.

There was something different this time. This was final. There would be no other opportunities to be loved and accepted into a family. The adoptive home had been his last chance. Despite his resentment against his adoptive parents and his fear of them, he had yearned with an infantile innocence to the very end for the abuse to cease and for his parents to love and accept him as their own. He desperately wanted to belong somewhere and to someone, to have a home and family he could trust, to be special to somebody. His need to survive had been sublimated, but not destroyed, this basic human need to be wanted. Aimlessly walking the streets alone that night he felt a deepened awareness of this need. Relief from finally being free of the abusive environment was not enough to overcome the more powerful feeling of repugnance he felt toward himself.

The sudden removal of the external danger around which he had built his existence left no outlet for his rage and hatred. In the days and months ahead they turned inward, unleashing themselves upon him with devastating effect. The threat of emotional self-destruction in the wake of physical deliverance became as real as had been the threat of the physical abuse itself. Though self-inflicted now, the abuse continued as Peter picked up where his parents left off.

The adoptive home had been his last chance. Now it and his parents were gone, like all the others. There would be no others. He had destroyed his last chance to be loved. And now he was on his own.

The agony and ecstasy of that awareness paralyzed Peter in a state of doubt and uncertainty. In utter despair he did not care whether he lived or died that night. The cost of caring was a price too high to pay.

Seeking oblivion, the rejected boy walked all night, unaware of where he was until at last the hardness of the bench pushed its way gradually into his consciousness. Peter looked around with eyes that only partially wanted to see. What he saw sent a chill racing down his spine. He was sitting in a pew in the church he had visited alone so many times. It was dark except for a dim light behind the cross at the altar. The large wooden cross hung in stark silhouette against the long backdrop behind the altar. Peter watched its dead stillness come alive as a symbol of renewed warmth and hope. Although he was alone in the church, Peter did not feel alone in the presence of that cross. It was real and permanent. As old as life itself. It was the beginning. To this day Peter cannot explain the strange, exhilarating warmth that spread slowly throughout his mind and body. In moments it had engulfed him like a cloak, thawing a heart turned stone against the cold of eternal oblivion. His body drew life from the warmth. His mind sought communion with the presence as real as his own, as though drawn irresistibly into the essence of that cross. Out of nowhere it came. A voice. Deep, gentle, compelling, speaking words that would resonate throughout the rest of his life.

*Out of the ruin and devastation of human tragedy
no less than my own, I offer you my greatest hope.*

After a moment more, Peter became aware of himself, sitting alone in the church in the dark, early hours of a morning soon to be transformed into day. As he became self-aware, the warmth began to dissipate. The presence left him. But the words remained. They never left him. In the dark, difficult days ahead, they remained his constant companion, always there, mysterious, like a coded message he could not decipher. Countless hours he would spend considering their possible meaning. Fifteen years later, Peter has begun to understand.

The warmth he felt in the church was replaced by a deep yearning to see the sun rise. Peter knew that it could not be far off. Walking rapidly with renewed purpose, Peter found himself near a pile of rocks in a familiar place. It was a jetty, a long pile of rocks protruding several hundred feet into the ocean which was designed to help break up the onrush of pounding waves so that the beaches would be safer for swimmers. He sat at the very end of it with his feet dangling in the seawater. Many times before, he had sat in this same spot. Like the special tree on the farm, this spot near the ocean was special to him. As the iridescent colors of a sun rushing to meet the morning began to streak across the sky, Peter sat with the lights of the city at his back. The significance of his position struck him. He was sitting at the center of the universe, at the point where the earth, sea, and sky all met. Despite feeling like a mistake that never should have happened . . . a flaw in the cosmic order . . . that not even beating could correct, Peter somehow felt at home in the midst of their meeting. For long moments he pondered the significance of where he sat and what was taking place around him. It was like the tree near the river where he and Bo would watch the sun rise. It was as though he had been removed from the world and given a special seat at the center of the universe from which to watch the dawning of a new day. Nothing else existed. Nothing else mattered at that moment. Just that he had been given the best seat in the house to witness the greatest and most important show on earth.

As the sun began to push itself above the furthest reaches of the ocean, Peter felt terribly alone. He wanted desperately for Bo to be cradled in his lap. To be able once again to share with him the joy of that sunrise. But the only thing he had left to cradle in his lap was his own hands, and they were empty.

Peter had no idea what he was going to do, how or where he was going to live. What about a job, school, transportation, clothes, food? Where could he sleep tonight? Where would he use the bathroom? At least in the adoptive home he had a place to stay out of the cold, food most of the time, a place to sleep, and his brothers. Now he had nothing. Nothing at all.

Gripped with fear and panic, Peter began to cry, softly at first, then in long, agonizing wails of grief. One wrenching sob after another tore painfully from his throat only to be swept away by the sea breeze to mingle unrecognizably among those of the gulls hovering in circles above the rocks.

Though the popular beach began to fill with people, Peter spent the morning alone in absolute solitude on the rocks. He wished that he could somehow be absorbed in the world around him . . . the earth and sea and sky . . . to somehow become a part of its predictable permanence. Just to exist without feeling.

There was comfort in that sunrise. Every morning of his life it had happened. The sun had risen. It rose again on this day despite all that had happened. Nothing had changed that. It was still the same. And it would stay the same. He could count on it.

The endless onrush of waves upon the beach was comforting. They never stopped coming one after another, hour after hour, day in and day out. Nothing could change that either.

No matter what happened during the day ahead of him, no matter how terrible it might be, the sun and waves would be there to greet him tomorrow morning. Like Bo. They would always be there. Nothing was going to change that. Nobody could take that away from him.

By noon the hunger pains were gnawing incessantly at Peter's consciousness. Enjoying the feel of the sun on his back and sand between his toes, he walked the half mile of beach that separated him from the pier. There was a snack shop there.

Trying to think about his health, he moved away from the row of candy bars. There was no nutritional value in candy bars. Finally, after minutes of indecision, Peter spent his thirty-five cents on a bag of popcorn. He felt good for having made such a healthy choice.

Soon the popcorn was gone. Temporarily satisfied, Peter sat watching the hundreds of people on the beach. He was fantasizing about what their lives must be like. No one noticed him. Or if they did, they paid him no attention.

Within hours Peter was hungry again. Having no money, he decided to look for a job. Beginning on the pier, he stopped at every store asking if they needed help. By late afternoon he had covered the length of the beach. No one needed help. Or if they did, he was too young.

Not yet concerned, Peter returned to the rocks as the sun began to dip below the horizon in a spectacular array of colors. He watched it appreciatively. It was not the first time he had gone a day without eating. But he was tired. So tired. He had not slept at all the night before. Thinking again of that night made him shiver.

Trying to make himself as comfortable as possible behind one of the larger rocks, using it to protect himself against the cool sea breeze blowing inland, the exhausted boy tried to relax. Within moments he was sound asleep.

But he did not sleep long. About midnight he awoke cold and shivering. He had to build a fire. Racing about the beach, he gathered driftwood to burn. In the sand around other burned-out campfires he found a half used box of matches and paper sacks he could use to start the fire. In a short time he had a small fire blazing in the rocks. In order to keep the fire going, Peter could only take catnaps throughout the night. Although what little sleep he did get helped, he was still groggy and sleepy the next morning.

He spent all of the second day looking for work. But it was the same story. Either they needed no help or they wanted him to be eighteen. The second night on the beach was worse than the first. It was colder. He was hungrier.

For two weeks it was the same thing over and over again. Peter tried everything he could think of to get a job. No one would hire him. For those two weeks he did not have a bite to eat, except for occasional scraps of hot dogs, popcorn, or other food remnants he could scavenge out of the garbage cans at the end of each day. The wadded up candy bar wrappers he found amongst the other trash in the garbage cans became the highlight of his days; there would almost always be some chocolate left on them. For some reason it never occurred to Peter to try to steal food from the snack shack or to lie about his age in order to get a job.

During those endless days ten thousand people must have seen Peter wandering alone and dejected on the beach, or seen his small campfire at night, or watched him curiously as he pawed methodically through the garbage cans. But not one person so much as asked the boy his name. It was as though he did not really exist, or that he was in another time dimension from them. No one seemed to notice or care.

He was afraid to approach anyone—afraid they would get angry at him or try to hurt him. They might think he was doing something wrong.

By the fourteenth day he was weak and sick. He had given up trying to find work several days before. It was no use. Needing all his energy just to find something to eat, Peter knew he was in deep trouble and desperately needed help.

On the morning of the fourteenth day, Peter watched again as the miracle of the sunrise played out before him. Even in his desperation he felt a tinge of joy at the sight. For a few moments the boy was allowed to forget his troubles as he lost himself in the majestic grandeur of the dawn unfolding before him. And then, out of nowhere, it came. A preacher's voice. A mother's smiling whisper. Like a gentle touch on the shoulder or a whiff of a familiar perfume, it came. Softly. Suddenly. A voice. Singing.

> Jesus loves me, this I know
> For the Bible tells me so. . . .

It was the rhyme he had sung so many times as a boy with Bo. It had been years since he had heard it. And now, suddenly, there it was. Why?

Maybe he was going crazy. Why not? He deserved to.

All morning long on that fourteenth day Peter tried to dismiss the tune from his mind. He tried to force his mind to pick out anything to think about that would crowd out those words. It was all a lie anyway. He was bad. Everyone knew that. His parents told him so. Thousands of times. He was so bad no one could possibly love him. He did not even deserve to be alive. If his mother and father couldn't love him, and his adoptive family hated him, how was it possible that Jesus could love him? It wasn't. Jesus loved good children. Children that didn't lie and make their parents angry. Children that were good so that their parents wanted to keep them. But Peter wasn't one of those children. He was bad, filth, scum, evil. Everyone hated him . . . even Jesus. . . .

Except Bo. Bo didn't hate him. Bo never treated him mean or hurt him. Bo loved him as much as he loved Bo.

The thought of Bo unfolded in his mind, countless memories of times spent with the only creature that ever really loved him. Peter was overwhelmed by a heart-breaking need to hold the animal in his lap just one more time, to feel his fur pressed against his cheek, to see those eager eyes watching and responding to his every move.

Suddenly the background of those memories was filled with that same tune, the one he had sung to the dog so many times in their long, lonely hours together. *"Jesus loves me, this I know . . . ."*

On and on it went. Peter no longer tried to stop it. A new thought came to the distraught boy. If Bo could love him. . . . After all, who knew him better than Bo? . . . then maybe, just maybe Jesus could love him too. Maybe it was true. Maybe someone really did love him.

As the thought played around in his mind, Peter decided that he was going to ask him. He was going to pray and ask Jesus to tell him if he really did love him or not. Prayer is how to talk to Jesus, and the boy suddenly wanted to talk to him.

Emptying his mind of thoughts, Peter tried hard to concentrate. It was hard. He had never made up his own prayer before. With his eyes closed, be began.

"Dear God . . ."

But that did not sound right. So he tried again.

"Hello, Jesus . . ."

That, too, did not sound right. He wanted desperately to say the right things so that Jesus would hear and pay attention to him. If he said the wrong thing, Jesus might get angry like his parents and think he was lying. The idea terrified him.

For over an hour Peter tried to find the right beginning to his prayer. He knew what he wanted to say, but he did not know how to say it in a way that would not be offensive. Over and over again he tried. Each time he became more frustrated. Finally, in despair, he burst out crying. "Please love me like Bo," he mumbled over and over as the tears washed his face of its frustration.

Several hours later as Peter was making his way painfully toward the garbage cans in a desperate search for something to eat, a motorcycle pulled up beside him. It was a chopper, the kind ridden by bikers. Several others pulled up behind the first.

"What the ——— you doin'?" the husky male voice asked.

Glancing at the man, Peter hardly recognized him because of his long hair, beard, and dark sunglasses. It was a kid he had known in school. Peter had felt sorry for him and they had become friends—sort of. No one had particularly liked him. He had acne. Hecklers constantly made fun of him and he would get angry and fight. He was kicked out of school numerous times, and finally he did not come back.

"Nuthin', Buck, what's happenin'?" Peter mumbled, moving away from the garbage can.

"Nuthin', huh? They finally kick you out?"

Peter had told him one time about his parents, when the curious boy had noticed the terrible bruises on his arms.

"Yeah, I guess so."

" 'Bout time you got away from that ——— place!" he exploded angrily, throttling the bike's powerful engine.

"Whatcha been up to, Buck?" Peter asked, trying to make conversation. "Still in school?"

"———no! That crap's for birds! Damn folks gave me the boot. Got me some friends here," he answered, nodding toward the bikers behind him with a smile.

There were six bikers in all. Two of the men had girls riding behind them. Peter looked at them silently. They were watching him. After a moment more of racing his engine, Buck returned his attention to Peter.

"Got a place to crash?"

"No."

"Well, don't just stand there. Get on!" Buck invited, smiling as he slid forward on the seat.

With nowhere else to go and no one else to turn to, Peter did not hesitate. As he got on the bike, he noticed the insignia on the back of Buck's vest. It was a picture of a red devil with horns. One fist held a pitchfork. The other was raised in a defiantly obscene gesture. The words above the insignia read "Satan's Saints."

As they rode away from the beach, Peter began to sense a new world opening to him. Life with the bikers was not what he had hoped for. But they wanted him. In the next few years they gave him a home, companionship, and a place to belong. He was important to them. They wanted him. That was enough.

[EPILOGUE]

[Hope for Tomorrow]

Peter Today

It must have been difficult for you to continue reading through one gruesome experience after another. Sensitive, compassionate people find no pleasure in others' misfortune, especially if that other is a child. I am grateful that you finished. However painful, it is important that we all experience the brutal reality that is child abuse from something other than a clinical perspective. For its prevention to be effective, its horror must be experienced at a personal level. Its pain is no less real than its brutality.

Peter's story did not end where I have concluded. There is much more to be shared. The effects of Peter's childhood experiences upon his life as an adolescent and young adult must also be considered in some detail if there is to be some appreciative understanding of just how devastating severe child abuse, short of death, can be. Perhaps this is the subject of another book.

Let me briefly sketch the remainder of Peter's story to the present.

I lived with the bikers for approximately two and a half years. Though I am not proud of that fact, it is as much an integral feature of my history as any other part. It cannot be overlooked or denied. Actually, the perspective I held by that time of life, and my place in it, fit nicely with the ethos of that particular subculture. I was a misfit, belonging nowhere but in the midst of other directionless misfits who held the same basic beliefs about themselves, other people, and the world.

I was no good, so I belonged with other no-goods. I was bad, even evil, so the life-style and activities of the group were a natural and expectable result. I was unloved and unwanted, so my acceptance in the group was assured. I put no trust in people or agents of authority and was, therefore, neatly aligned with the rebellious, antiauthoritarian stance of my comrades. Violence and intimidation were the altar around which we all gathered, with the hope of attaining the power over ourselves and others it promised but never supplied. And yet, we continually turned to it as the basis of all relationships exterior to the group. At times it gave us what we wanted, or thought we wanted. But in its wake came the law, pressing us endlessly for the one mistake that would deliver us into the hands of the criminal justice system. We were outlaws, existing on the fringes of society, at a level of such social and personal degradation that the fine line between human and animal became obscure. As a biker I, like the rest of them, lived for two basic purposes: pain avoidance and immediate gratification. Negative experiences, unless they could be controlled by brute strength and numbers, were ignored, denied, or avoided. Pleasures were sought, created, taken, often ruthlessly and at others' expense, whenever available. No questions asked. No justification necessary. No serious afterthoughts. Moment by moment, day by day we lived, moving from one experience to another in an unending search for fulfillment.

A group of eight men and three women lived together in a slumlike two-bedroom apartment, its filth and physical chaos mirroring the lives and thinking of its inhabitants. Sleep, food, sex, and drugs—the essentials of life—were communal, taken when wanted. No routine. Based on animal instincts.

Each member was expected to chip in his share of money to support the life and style of the group. How it was derived was unimportant. I got a part-time job as a busboy in an exclusive restaurant.

For a reason I still do not understand, I forced myself to complete my senior year of high school and graduate with the rest of the class. It was hard. There were many diversions. Countless times the urge to drop out became almost overpowering. The high school diploma seemed far beyond my reach, an unrealistic, unattainable goal. But, I made it. Somehow I made it. I graduated with my class. Why it was so important to me, I really do not know. Perhaps it was the only semblance of normalcy left in my life—a stolen piece of the "good" life maybe. I wanted to be like the other kids in school, to live like them, and school was the only part of my life over which I felt I had control. Control, that is, only so long as the authorities remained unaware of my changed situation.

For whatever reason, I did finish high school. The next couple of years I drifted, moving from one meaningless job after another, avoiding responsibilities whenever possible, taking pleasures wherever I could find them. Nothing meant anything to me. I had nothing to live for except to avoid arrest, which I was fairly successful at doing. Though I was arrested several times on suspicion of this or that, nothing could ever be proved and I was always released to continue my journey into self-destruction.

It was a lonely, empty, meaningless way to live. But it was all I had. The bikers were all I had. They were all I deserved.

After I was gone from my adoptive home, things got better for my baby brothers. The beatings stopped. My parents bought them a car. And they were allowed to be teenagers. Both graduated from high school and immediately began careers as enlisted men in the Marine Corps.

A hundred times during my first year away from home, I tried to enlist in the service. It was during the Vietnam War. I really wanted to be a marine, but would settle for any branch that would take me. I not only wanted the security it offered, but even more I wanted to kill somebody. And I wanted it to be a slow, agonizing death. I wanted someone else to hurt as badly as I had hurt. Thankfully, out of those hundred applications and countless physicals, I received an equal number of rejections. I was to survive on the street or die. I chose to survive.

My desire to survive came dramatically to the forefront one evening on a deserted beach. We were on a run, wearing our colors. The two combined meant only one thing: we were looking for trouble. We found it. Another gang, wearing their colors, were partying on the beach. We stopped. They came forward with knives and chains. We met them more than halfway. It was instant ignition.

When the battle was over, one of our own lay dead where he had fallen, his face crushed by a blow from a lead pipe. He happened to be my "best friend" in the group. His death—the inevitable end of us all and our lifestyle—so shocked me that I spent the better part of that night sitting alone on a hill overlooking the battle scene. I knew that it could just as easily have been me lying dead on that beach. I also knew, though this was the first time I had admitted it, that my life orientation was leading me in the direction of a mental institution, a prison, or a graveyard. No other end was possible. I did not want any of the three. I knew that something better was possible. And I vowed that night to find it. How or where or when, I had no idea. But I decided to do it, somehow. I had lived through hell once. I did not want to be sentenced by my own choices to another tour.

At the age of twenty I met my future wife. To this day I cannot understand what she possibly could have seen in me that was promising. The way I lived, the way I thought and behaved, my values, my perceptions of life, people, and reality—all were distorted, adapted for survival in a hostile, life-threatening environment, totally self-destructive under any other conditions.

Because of my experiences with mother-figure women, I could not believe that she actually loved me, the man, the person. Despite my doubts and fears, we were married after a brief engagement.

She gave me something to live for, to feel good about. I

entered junior college. Six weeks later I flunked out. The following semester I reapplied. I was able to convince the reluctant admissions officer to readmit me on probation. I barely survived the semester—but I did. I stayed on probation for another year, barely making a C average. By then I had adjusted adequately to being married and being around nonthreatening people in a nonthreatening environment, and had a fairly decent job through a work/study program sponsored by the school. Four years later I graduated with an associate of arts degree. What an achievement! I was so excited.

Sure of being rejected, but somehow willing to take the risk, I applied for admission to a state college as an upper division student.

Much to my amazement I was accepted. To have the opportunity to earn a bachelor's degree was beyond my wildest dreams. Already I had surpassed the limits of my own envisioned capabilities.

Moving the family, I worked at odd jobs while attending school. Both my son and daughter were born during this time. I graduated with a bachelor's degree in English in 1974.

Convinced by a minister at the church I attended irregularly that God had built his Kingdom on human, ordinary men and women with backgrounds as tainted and soiled as my own, I dared to acknowledge a call to the ministry. Such audacity for an ex-biker! In the fall of 1975, I entered a southern seminary. I graduated with a master's degree three years later.

Continuing to doubt my own adequacy, I resigned my ordination candidacy and entered a doctoral program at a major southern university. Within a year after graduation from seminary, my wife left me. She had had enough. I do not blame her. The life I had provided was anything but what she had hoped for. She deserved so much more.

I am single now, still living near enough my children to see them several times a week. They are the most important people in my life. I have vowed not to allow to happen to them what happened to me. They will know their father. He will be there. Like Bo for me, I will always be there for them.

I completed the doctoral program in 1982 and am now working with ICARE as a public and professional educator in the area of child abuse, neglect, and incest. (ICARE—International Child Advocacy and Resource Enterprises—is a child advocacy program focusing on the prevention and treatment of child abuse through education and therapeutic intervention.) In most respects I am a happy, stable, well-adjusted person, though impatient at times. I must be alert constantly for signals of my self-destructive tendency becoming operative again. It is still there. Though I have come a long way, I still have far to go.

I suppose that I will live the rest of my life as a deprived, abused child. But now, hopefully, I can also live it as a fulfilled adult, blessed with life and opportunity.

Child Abuse: A Survey of the Problem

Throughout history infancy has been a dangerous time of life and it remains so for thousands of children in our country even today. Infanticide, infant torture, incest, and abandonment are all extreme forms of child abuse which continue to be documented daily as an integral feature in the social history of the human race.

Childrearing has traditionally been a private, family matter. In our society, parents and other family members have cared for and disciplined their children by whatever means they chose with a minimum of outside awareness or interference. As a result, family violence and abuse have been considered and kept family secrets.

However, times have changed. The wall of secrecy surrounding family childrearing practices is being breeched by a growing awareness in the general public of the shocking incidence and degree of child maltreatment in this country. There is a growing concern that children must be protected from harm and danger regardless of its source. That children have an equal right to protection under the law may seem obvious to most people. The sad truth is that such protection has been provided only recently in this country. Even then, it is tenuous protection at best. The laws are usually applied after the fact—after the abuse has occurred in most instances. In many cases, that is too late. The damage is done.

How extensive is the problem of child abuse in this country? Many researchers believe child abuse is a leading cause of infant mortality in the United States, and they estimate that nearly one million American children are suffering from some form of abuse or neglect in their homes at any given time. Moreover, approximately one quarter of those children will be injured permanently or handicapped for life as a result of their maltreatment. Though statistics are imprecise, an estimated five thousand children will die at the hands of their parents or guardians this year in our country.[1] Some have referred to child abuse and neglect as an epidemic of massive proportions with devastating consequences not only for the victim and his family, but for society as well.

What is child abuse and neglect? The words *child abuse* and *child neglect* mean different things to different people in different situations and cultures. The difficulty of arriving at a generally acceptable definition becomes apparent when only a few of the many perspectives are considered. A physician, for example, will tend to view child abuse as a medical problem in need of diagnosis and treatment. A law enforcement officer, on the other hand, will tend to view it as criminal conduct to be detected and arrested. To an attorney, child abuse may represent violation of basic human, legal, and constitutional rights, whereas a clergyman might see it in terms of the violation of the sanctity of human life. To a sociologist, child abuse may represent social and family dysfunction, while to a psychiatrist it may be a symptom of personality aberration in need of psychotherapy. A moralist may view it as monstrous and unnatural acts, while to a philosopher it may represent the epitome of "man's inhumanity to man." Each perspective encompasses an element of truth but recognizes only a particular dimension of the problem.

Prevailing definitions seem to many professionals both too broad and too narrow. It is difficult to draft legislation which is specific enough to prevent improper or indiscriminate application and yet broad enough to cover situations of harm to a child.[2]

Parallels exist between attempts at defining child abuse and defining other types of social behavior, such as aggression. Each have inherent ambiguities arising out of the judgments or inferences of the observer concerning the perpetrator's intentions. Intentionality is one of two primary approaches to a definition. However, this approach involves more than an observable act or sequence of behavior which can be measured reliably. The validity of individual judgments of intentionality is highly questionable in any court of law. Thus, utilizing intentionality as the basis of a definition raises serious problems. The other approach is to define child abuse in terms of its outcome, which serves to focus attention upon the injured child rather than the perpetrator's motives. The obvious problem with this approach is that accidental injuries are grouped with intentionally inflicted injuries. To date these problems have yet to be resolved and a clearly acceptable definition of child abuse and neglect proposed.[3] As a result, the federal government has proposed a generally acceptable legal definition as a guideline, leaving specific definition to the states and counties.

On January 31, 1974, the Ninety-third Congress of the United States passed the Child Abuse Prevention and Treatment Act (P.L. No. 93–247). The act established for the first time within the federal government a National Center on Child Abuse and Neglect, located in Washington, D.C. In addition, the act defined child abuse and neglect as, "The physical or mental injury, sexual abuse, negligent treatment, or maltreatment of a child under the age of eighteen by a person who is responsible for the child's welfare under circumstances which indicate that the child's health or welfare is harmed or threatened thereby."[4]

Despite cultural variations there are norms of acceptable child care in this country. Since the 1960s all fifty states, the District of Columbia, the Virgin Islands, Puerto Rico, and Guam have enacted laws to protect children whose parents fail to meet minimal standards of care. Although child abuse and neglect laws vary state to state, there are certain provisions that remain relatively constant among the laws of all states. All statutes, for example, stipulate the kinds of maltreatment that must be reported to government agencies.[5]

Four primary maltreatment categories are now recognized in reporting laws:
1. Physical abuse—the nonaccidental physical injury of a child;
2. Physical neglect—the failure to supply the essentials of life to a child;
3. Sexual abuse—the sexual exploitation of a child; and,
4. Emotional abuse—the infliction of psychological or emotional injury upon a child.[6]

In a paper published by the Regional Institute of Social Welfare Research in Athens, Georgia, two additional types of child maltreatment were identified. The first is verbal abuse. Just as physical injuries can scar and incapacitate a child, emotional cruelty through verbal assaults, such as belittling or blaming language, sarcasm, unpredictable parental responses, continual negative moods, constant family discord, and double message communication, can similarly cripple or handicap a child emotionally, behaviorally, and intellectually. The second is emotional deprivation. This deprivation is suffered by children when their parents do not provide the normal and necessary feelings of being loved, wanted, secure, and worthy. Children need emotional nurturing and involvement from their parents for normal development as much as they need proper and adequate nutrition. Emotional starvation is one of the most difficult abuses to detect and is, perhaps, the most tragic.[7]

Researchers Wayne Holder and Patricia Schene discuss four additional types of child abuse:

1. Moral neglect—occurs when a child is subjected to influences which have or may corrupt the child;
2. Medical neglect—occurs when the child's need for medical care is ignored;
3. Educational neglect—occurs when there is failure to provide the education required by law; and,
4. Community neglect—occurs when the community fails to provide the support and services necessary to insure the health and welfare of all children.[8]

In her book entitled *Breaking the Cycle of Child Abuse*, Christine Herbruck identifies yet another type of child maltreatment which she claims is as pernicious as the rest. She calls it "passive abuse." The passive abuser never actually lays a hand on the child, but is just as involved in the abuse as if personally administering it. The passive abuser paves the way for abuse, sets it up, and allows it to occur. Instead of acting out feelings, the passive abuser manipulates someone else into acting them out.[9]

One of the most hotly contested issues in the child abuse debate is the question of whether corporal punishment is child abuse. The Regional Institute of Social Welfare Research concluded that the most common cause of inflicted injury upon children is overpunishment which occurs when corporal punishment is unreasonably severe. The combination of physical punishment and rage, they note, can be deadly.[10]

Researchers Ross Parke and Candace Collmer point out, however, that it would not be useful to adopt a definition of child abuse which includes corporal punishment. In a survey of parents, ninety-three percent admitted using corporal punishment in the rearing of their children, while present statistics suggest only four percent of the population in this country is subject to abuse. It is questionable, they concluded, whether a definition which includes over ninety percent of the population is sufficiently discriminatory to be effective.[11]

The problem of defining exactly what constitutes child

abuse is a difficult and perhaps insurmountable one, particularly in a culture which condones the use of violence in recreation, discipline, and relationships. A society rooted in violence cannot hope to be free of violence, even against its children.

The debate rages on and children continue to die. Few surviving victims of severe child abuse would have as much difficulty defining it.

What causes parents to abuse their children? "Human history has woven through it like a scarlet thread the need and importance of a scapegoat, someone to blame, someone to carry the responsibility for the unpreventable and unprevented misfortunes of life, someone to sacrifice to appease those dark forces which disturb human security, someone who can be hated and destroyed with justification as intrinsically evil. Whether that someone be a harmless woman hanged as a witch in Salem, a Jew in Nazi Germany, or a child in an abusing family, he is himself crushed under the weight of human madness."[12]

This is one perspective concerning the cause of child abuse. There are others.

Though the issue of causality is extremely complex and multifaceted, research indicates that there is a higher probability that child abuse will occur in a family when the following basic conditions are met:

1. There is an increased potential for abuse in one or both parents. The potential for abuse is heightened by such dynamics as social and emotional isolation, low self-esteem, inability to meet personal needs, inability or unwillingness to seek help, severe marital difficulties, unrealistic expectations of children, and parents who have themselves been victims of abuse.

2. The child is viewed as being a problem or different from other children. This occurs most often when the child is unwanted, premature, handicapped, or a problem delivery. Sometimes a child is experienced as an unwelcome intrusion into the family or as a projection of the more unacceptable qualities of the

parent or other family member, or has special needs requiring special care, attention, or effort on the part of the parent.

3. There is a crisis or series of crises in the family. The crisis need not be major, but is experienced by the parent as personal failure, helplessness, and rejection. Feelings of powerlessness often experienced in crisis generally precede and help precipitate the incident of abuse.[13]

To gain a thorough understanding of the etiology of child abuse, all forces at work upon, within, and without the individual and family must be considered. There are no easy answers or solutions. Only the tragic results of child abuse are easy.

What kind of persons abuse their child? The National Committee for the Prevention of Child Abuse in their pamphlet entitled "It Shouldn't Hurt to Be a Child" describes the abusive parents this way:

> Abusers are friends, neighbors, and relatives. It is a sad irony that many abusers genuinely love their children, but find themselves caught in life situations beyond their control and they do not know how to cope. They are often isolated from friends and family and may have no one to give them emotional support. They may not like themselves and may not know how to get their emotional needs met. All abused children do not grow up to be abusive parents, though many do. Because abusive parenting is all they know, they repeat it with their own children.
>
> Abusers often perceive a child as being different or having special needs that set the child apart from other children. Perhaps the child was illegitimate, the result of an unplanned pregnancy, and/or a difficult birth, or wanted for the wrong reasons. Sometimes the child's mannerisms or behavior reminds the parent of his or her own childhood self or of another adult who the parent now dislikes. Sometimes there are very real special needs that set the child apart from other children such as physical handicap, mental retardation, or a chronic illness. Sometimes in a family of several children, just one will be singled out as a victim while the others lead relatively normal lives. In other cases, all the children will be abused.

Abusers tend to have unrealistic or inappropriate expectations of their children. They may set standards that are impossibly high.

Child abuse does not belong solely in the domain of the poor. Abusers come from all economic, racial, social, and religious groups. Life stresses such as money problems, marital difficulties, and unemployment do contribute to the potential for abuse. But why some parents under heavy stress abuse their children and others in similar circumstances do not is a very complex issue that is not yet fully understood.

Whether it be one stressful circumstance or a number of crises that actually trigger abuse, it is clear that a combination of factors build so that a person simply cannot cope any longer. Violence becomes a defense mechanism and children its target.[14]

What are the consequences of child abuse? The effects of severe child abuse are devastating; the consequences, tragic. Reaching beyond the life of the victim, the family and society are affected as well.

Crime in the streets begins with violence in the home. When violence becomes normative in the family as a means to control, dominate, or resolve conflict, children tend to adopt it as a power source in their own relationships. The result is often delinquency and criminality on the streets, particularly crimes against persons. A large number of our rapists and murderers come from violent and abusive homes.

Abusive parents create for themselves and their children an environment balanced precariously between disaster and tragedy. They live constantly on the threshold of self-destruction.

Chronically abusive families are generally characterized by instability, deprivation, unpredictability, marital conflict, danger, and violence. Such an environment is not conducive to healthy growth and development of children or adults. The result of child abuse in these families is often the breakup of the family: the death of a child, imprisonment for one or both parents, divorce, children left in the custody of the state, or long periods of separation and institutional supervision while family rehabilitation is attempted. In any case, every member of the family suffers when a child is abused in the home.

Institutional dependency often characterizes the adult lives of many child abuse victims. Prisons, psychiatric hospitals, and unemployment and welfare offices become institutional parents providing basic human needs for those who cannot seem to survive without help. The maintenance expense of these life support systems is awesome and a burden to every taxpayer.

Whether from aggression in the streets, families torn apart, or institutional dependency, all of society suffers along with the victim and family when a child is beaten and abused in the home. Society suffers and society pays.

The cost to society is nominal, however, when compared to the horror and agony of helpless children unable to defend themselves from every imaginable torture at the hands of their parents. For them, the full weight of human madness crashes into their young lives for no apparent reason, leaving them dead, disfigured, crippled, handicapped, or impaired. If they are fortunate enough to survive physically, many tend to develop as social mutants and survive emotionally as living distortions of normalcy. An endless, repressed rage propels many of them into a life-style of violence, degradation, and self-destruction. Prisons, mental institutions, and graveyards claim most of these at an early age.

Those able to avoid self-destruction cannot escape the horrifying memories of a resurging past; a past so terrible in many cases that it can neither be confronted nor ignored. At one level of awareness or another, its evil pervades every living moment of every dying day.

Many survivors of severe abuse become slaves to their past. They become chained emotionally to past abusive events, and their victimization is perpetuated into their adult lives and the lives of their children. As a result of the abuse, many children grow into adults believing the world to be a dangerous and hostile place where people cannot be trusted, particularly those in authority; where avoiding pain means avoiding the very relationships they need so desperately. Many believe they are inherently bad or evil, and therefore unlovable, actually deserving the often hideous atrocities inflicted upon them as children. Most believe they are worthless failures, possessing no right to life and happiness. Even worse, many grow up believing that no one gives a damn.

For people with such a distorted view of reality, the best that they can hope for is survival in a life twisted and distorted into a bizarre reflection of what it could be. Sociopathology, criminal activities, addiction, promiscuity, imprisonment, suicide, divorce, unemployment, failure, hopelessness, and despair often characterize the life-sweeping aftermath of chronic and severe child abuse.

The pain and suffering caused by child abuse do not end with the final blow. Although the body may heal and show only scars, the heart and mind of a child is far more fragile and vulnerable. The emotional damage resulting from even one incident of severe abuse may take years to overcome. I know, because I am a survivor of severe child abuse.

I, like so many other victims, evolved into a sociopath and adopted a life-style that very nearly accomplished what my parents could not—my destruction. Almost. But not quite.

I survived long enough to realize that my right to life is no less than your own, that I did not deserve the abuse inflicted upon me, and that as an adult I no longer have to be a slave to the horror of my childood. I now have a choice, a choice of life-style, content, and purpose. Though I continue to pay dearly for having once been a child, I am no longer a living, perpetual sacrifice to human madness. I have broken the cycle of abuse in my life and can now turn my attention to a life of meaning, purpose, and fulfillment with my own children.

Many are not so fortunate. The cycle of abuse is perpetuated into their adult lives. The cycle seems endless, hopeless to stop or prevent. Robbed of their childhoods, many survive only to find their adult years stolen away by an equal tragedy of a different sort. The suffering continues, endlessly. For many, life becomes what they do while they are waiting to die. If only they can survive that long.

[Notes]

1. California Department of Justice, *The Problem of the Abused and Neglected Child* (California: Department of Justice, 1976), p. 6
2. National Center on Child Abuse and Neglect, *Child Abuse and Neglect: The Problem and Its Management* (Washington, D.C.: U.S. Department of Health, Education, and Welfare, 1978), p. 3.
3. Ibid.
4. National Center on Child Abuse and Neglect, *Early Childhood Programs and the Prevention and Treatment of Child Abuse and Neglect* (Washington, D.C.: U.S. Department of Health, Education, and Welfare, 1979), p. 1.
5. National Center on Child Abuse and Neglect, *Child Abuse and Neglect*, p. 29.
6. Michael Halperin, *Helping Maltreated Children* (London: The C. V. Mosby Company, 1979), p. 17.
7. Regional Institute of Social Welfare Research, *Child Abuse is Scary: Facts and Feelings For Those Who May Need to Report* (Athens, Ga.: Regional Institute of Social Welfare Research, 1979), p. 1.
8. Wayne M. Holder and Patricia Schene, *Understanding Child Neglect and Abuse* (Colorado: American Humane Association, Child Protection, 1978), p. 3.
9. Christine Comstock Herbruck, *Breaking the Cycle of Child Abuse* (Minneapolis: Winston Press, 1979), p. 25.
10. Regional Institute of Social Welfare Research, *Child Abuse Is Scary*, p. 2.
11. Ross D. Parke and Candace W. Collmer, "Child Abuse: An Interdisciplinary Analysis," in *Review of Child Development Research*, ed. E. Hetherington, vol. 5 (Chicago: University of Chicago Press, 1975), p. 513.

12. Leontine Young, *Wednesday's Children* (New York: McGraw-Hill, 1964) p. 52.
13. National Committee for Prevention of Child Abuse, *Think You Know Something About Child Abuse?* (Chicago: National Committee for Prevention of Child Abuse, 1977), p. 1.
14. National Committee for Prevention of Child Abuse, "It Should Not Hurt to Be a Child" (Chicago: National Committee for Prevention of Child Abuse, 1982), p. 6.

[What You Can Do to Help]

Early detection is essential in the prevention and treatment of child abuse. Child abuse is rarely episodic. Its frequency and intensity increase over time. The longer it goes unrecognized and untreated, the more devastating its effects and the harder it becomes to treat. Actualized cases of abuse must be stopped immediately, before it is too late. Potential instances of abuse must be prevented. Failure in this regard may not only destroy a family, it may cost the life of a child.

There are many ways you can help prevent this unnecessary tragedy. But it begins with you. Make sure your own children grow up in an environment free of abuse and its threat. Reach out for help if you think you need it. Being a parent is not an easy task for anyone. Do not wait until there is a tragedy in your family to get help. By then it may be too late.

If you are parents of young children, or are just now planning your family, prepare for parenthood. Take parenting and child development classes. Learn parenting and coping skills. Learn what reasonable expectations you can have of your children at particular ages. Realize from the beginning that parenting is a job—a difficult task— which could be made easier and more effective with some training. Care enough about your children to learn how to be good and successful parents.

Make a rational, informed decision concerning the use

and exercise of corporal punishment in relationship with your children. Keep in mind that violence tends to perpetuate violence. Learn alternative disciplinary methods. Understand the difference between punishment, which is nothing more or less than revenge, and discipline, which is teaching out of love and respect for the child as a human being.

Pay attention to your own needs. Make sure they are being met in constructive, adult relationships. Avoid the trap of isolation and estrangement from life and people. People need people. So do you.

Assured of the health and well-being of your own family, reach out to neighbors, friends, and relatives. Visit people in their own homes. Sometimes just breaking the barrier of silence and aloneness is all it takes to prevent an incident of child abuse.

Be sensitive to signals of individual or family distress. Be a caring friend. Listen. Especially listen to children. Few children are capable of fantasizing abuse. Find ways to help a family cope with the stresses which provide the fuel for violence in the home. Become a "lifeline" for the family. Know what and where family resources are available in your community. Get involved. Care.

Most important, report to the appropriate agency any cases of suspected child abuse. You do not need to be sure. Suspicion is all that is necessary. Report. Do not become a passive accomplice in the beating and torture of a child. His or her life may depend on your phone call to the intervention agency. A report can be made anonymously. You need not identify yourself. Speak up for the child who cannot help himself.

Other ways to help prevent child abuse are to volunteer your time and money. Helping agencies are always in need of volunteer help and contributions. There is a real need for public awareness and education programs. Get involved.

If you belong to a professional group which has regular contact with children, make sure you and the other members are trained to recognize the symptoms of child abuse, both in parents and children. There are many. Sponsor a training seminar. Attend a lecture. Visit your library. There is an increasing volume of literature in the area. Ignorance in this area is inexcusable, perhaps deadly.

Be careful that you do not fall victim to one or another of the negative cultural perspectives of childhood which are so popular even today. Childhood is not an inferior condition which must be overcome. Children are not little adults. There is no need to "beat the devil" out of any child. Sparing the rod will not spoil the child. Let your children be children in the fullness of childhood. Childhood is a stage of human development which should be enjoyed and experienced to the fullest. The freedom to be a child—happy, wanted, loved, and secure—is the greatest gift you as a parent can give your child. Give it—with love.

If you should want or need more information concerning how you can help prevent child abuse in your own family and community, please write to me in care of the publisher. I will get your letter. And I promise to answer it.

[Conclusion]

Parents are the gods of children. A young child can know no other. Possessing absolute authority, they have the power to build or destroy, to mold or bind, to strengthen or weaken, to bless or curse, to give life or to bring death. When the church speaks of God's love and acceptance, it has no meaning for the young child apart from the love and acceptance of his or her parents. If there is hate, rejection, pain, distress, and chaos at home, the child learns early the emptiness of words proclaimed as gospel from the pulpit. Jesus becomes a grotesque image of mystery, myth, and meaninglessness. God becomes a word used to curse.

As an adult survivor of six years of severe child abuse—both physical and emotional—I often wonder why the church did nothing to help me, my brothers, and my parents. Was it that they could not see the bruises, the cuts, scratches, and abrasions covering my body? Could they not see the desperation out of which my parents lived? Or the need? Surely as I attended church school classes someone must have noticed the pain and terror in my eyes, the hopelessness with which I moved, my withdrawal into isolation, or, at least, the swelling in my hands and feet. Surely someone must have noticed me.

The priest was often in our home socially, as were other members of the church. Relatives were also there frequently. Could they not see what was happening to me?

Surely the neighbors heard my screams in the middle of the night. Were they too frightened to help me? Did not the teachers at school wonder why I was so passive and withdrawn? Why didn't the police begin to suspect something when I ran away from home so many times?

For six years I was beaten and battered by my parents. For six years I was ignored by everyone who came into contact with me. I would have given anything during that time if my prayers to God for help had been answered. But God was silent, his people were silent, and I suffered in silence. But no more! Please join me and others in crying out for mercy and compassion on behalf of all children, everywhere. Speak up, learn, get involved. Our children need us desperately. Even more, we need our children—healthy and alive.

[Bibliography]

Bakan, David. *Slaughter of the Innocents*. San Francisco: Jossey-Bass Publishers, 1976.

Fontana, Vincent J. *Somewhere A Child Is Crying*. New York: MacMillan Publishing Company, 1973.

Herbruck, Christine Comstock. *Breaking the Cycle of Child Abuse*. Minneapolis: Winston Press, 1979.

Kempe, C. Henry, and Helfer, Ray E., eds. *Helping the Battered Child and His Family*. Philadelphia: J. B. Lippincott Company, 1972.

Kempe, Ruth S., and Kempe, C. Henry. *Child Abuse*. Cambridge, Mass.: Harvard University Press, 1978.

Walters, David R. *Physical and Sexual Abuse of Children: Causes and Treatment*. Bloomington: Indiana University Press, 1975.

Young, Leontine. *Wednesday's Children*. New York: McGraw-Hill, 1964.

[Regional Child Abuse and Neglect Resource Centers]

Region 1 CA/N Resource Center
Judge Baker Guidance Center
295 Longwood Avenue
Boston, Massachusetts 02115

617-232-8390

(CT, ME, MA, RI, VT, NH)

* * * *

Region II CA/N Resource Center
College of Human Ecology
Cornell University
MVR Hall
Ithaca, New York 14853

607-256-7794

(NJ, NY, PR, VI)

* * * *

Region III CA/N Resource Center
Howard University Institute for
Urban Affairs and Research
P.O. Box 191
Washington, D.C. 20059

202-686-6770

(DC, DE, MD, PA, VA, WV)

Region IV CA/N Resource Center
Regional Institute for Social
Welfare Research
P.O. Box 152
Athens, Georgia 30601

404-542-7614
(AL, FL, GA, KY, MS, NC, SC, TN)

* * * *

Region V CA/N Resource Center
Graduate School of Social Work
University of Wisconsin-Milwaukee
Milwaukee, Wisconsin 53201

414-963-4184
(IL, IN, MI, MN, OH, WI)

* * * *

Region VI CA/N Resource Center
Graduate School of Social Work
University of Texas at Austin
Austin, Texas 78712

512-471-4067
(AR, LA, NM, OK, TX)

* * * *

Region VII CA/N Resource Center
Institute of Child Behavior
and Development
University of Iowa—Oakdale Campus
Oakdale, Iowa 52319

319-353-4825
(IA, KS, MO, NE)

Region VIII CA/N Resource Center
National Center for the Prevention
and Treatment of CA/N
1205 Oneida Street
Denver, Colorado 80220
303-321-3963
(CO, MT, ND, SD, UT, WY)

* * * *

Region IX CA/N Resource Center
Department of Special Education
California State University
5151 State University Drive
Los Angeles, California 90032
213-224-3283
(AZ, CA, HI, NV, Guam, Trust Terr.)

* * * *

Region X CA/N Resource Center
Western Federation for Human Services
157 Yesler Way, #208
Seattle, Washington 98104
206-624-5480
(AK, ID, OR, WA)